1599   Moved to Southwark near the Globe Theatre which he and his company had recently erected.

1602   Extensive purchases of property and land in Stratford.

1602–4   Lodged with Mountjoy, a Huguenot refugee and a maker of headdresses, in Cripplegate, London. Helped to arrange a marriage between Mary Mountjoy and Stephen Belott, her father's apprentice.

1603   His company became the King's Majesty's Players under royal patronage.

1607   His daughter Susanna married Dr John Hall.

1608   Birth of Shakespeare's grand-daughter Elizabeth Hall.

1610   Shakespeare possibly returned to live in Stratford.

1613   Purchase of the Gatehouse in Blackfriars. Burning of the Globe Theatre during the première of *Henry VIII*.

1616   Marriage of his daughter Judith to Thomas Quiney in Lent for which they were excommunicated.

25 March, 1616   Shakespeare altered the draft of his will presumably to give Judith more security in view of her husband's unreliability and his pre-marital misconduct with another woman. His will also revealed his strong attachment to his Stratford friends, and above all his desire to arrange for the establishment of his descendants.

23 April, 1616   Death of Shakespeare.

1623   Publication of the First Folio edition of Shakespeare's plays collected by his fellow actors Heminge and Con___ _____ ___ _____ __ _o worthy a friend'

D0997053

G. DEPT.

THE
TEMPEST

The Players' Shakespeare

MACBETH

TWELFTH NIGHT

THE MERCHANT OF VENICE

KING HENRY IV PART ONE

JULIUS CÆSAR

A MIDSUMMER NIGHT'S DREAM

AS YOU LIKE IT

HENRY V

ROMEO AND JULIET

ANTONY AND CLEOPATRA

HAMLET

OTHELLO

RICHARD II

Also edited by Dr J. H. Walter

HENRY V (Arden Shakespeare)

CHARLEMAGNE (Malone Society)

LAUNCHING OF THE MARY (Malone Society)

THE
TEMPEST

Edited by
J. H. WALTER
M.A., PH.D.

Formerly Headmaster
Minchenden School, Southgate
Fellow of University College, London

HEINEMANN
EDUCATIONAL

Heinemann Educational Books Ltd
Halley Court, Jordan Hill, Oxford OX2 8EJ

OXFORD   LONDON   EDINBURGH
MADRID   ATHENS   BOLOGNA   PARIS
MELBOURNE   SYDNEY   AUCKLAND
IBADAN   NAIROBI   HARARE   GABORONE
SINGAPORE   TOKYO   PORTSMOUTH NH (USA)

ISBN 0 435 19007 5

93 94 95 15 14 13 12 11 10 9 8 7

Printed in England by Clays Ltd, St Ives plc

CONTENTS

PREFACE   *page* 1

INTRODUCTION   3

THE TEMPEST   31

APPENDICES:

   I Note on the Date of the Play   185
  II Influence of the Æneid   186
 III Notes on Some of the Songs and Music   188
 IV Shakespeare's Theatre   189

PREFACE

THE aim of this edition is to encourage pupils to study the play as a play, to see it not so much as a novel or a narrative, but as a pattern of speech and movement creating an artistic whole. While it has been generally accepted that this approach stimulates and enlivens classroom work, it has more recently become clear that it is a most fruitful way of preparing for examinations. The recent reports issued by the Cambridge Local Examinations Syndicate call attention to this aspect in the work of both Ordinary Level and Advanced Level candidates. The following comments are taken from the Advanced Level report:

'It will be seen that the best candidates are often those who show themselves conscious of the play as a made thing—usually, but by no means, always, as a thing made for the theatre' (p. 5). Again, 'And perhaps the most misunderstood aspect of Shakespeare is the part played by theatrical convention . . .' (p. 6).

The interleaved notes, therefore, contain, in addition to a gloss, interpretations of character, dialogue, and imagery, considered particularly from the point of view of a play. There are some suggestions for acting, for the most part simple pointers to avoid rigidity of interpretation and drawn up with an apron stage in mind. Some questions are interposed to provide topics for discussion or to assist in discrimination.

It is suggested that the play should be read through rapidly with as little comment as possible. On a second reading the notes should be used in detail, and appropriate sections of the Introduction might be read at the teacher's discretion.

It is hoped that this edition will enable the teacher to take his class more deeply into the play than the usual meagre allowance of time permits him to do; it is not an attempt to usurp his function.

The play was first published in the First Folio, 1623. I have also consulted the modern editions of C. J. Sisson, Sir Arthur Quiller-Couch and J. Dover Wilson, F. Kermode, and Northrop Frye. References to Shakespeare's plays not yet published in this edition are to the Tudor Edition, edited by P. Alexander, 1951. The text printed here is complete.

Preface

No consideration has been given in the Introduction to the theories of a text reconstituted for an early play by Shakespeare, or of matter excised in order to insert the masque for the performance at Whitehall during the wedding festivities of Princess Elizabeth. There are some inconsistencies that may indicate alterations and changes of mind, but the play acts as a unified whole.

I am very much indebted to a number of standard works by Chambers, Greg, Baldwin, and G. Wilson Knight.

The following among others have proved most helpful: D. C. Allen, *Image and Meaning*; R. A. Brower, *The Fields of Light*; W. C. Curry, *Shakespeare's Philosophical Patterns*; L. Kirschbaum, *Two Lectures on Shakespeare*; P. O. Kristeller, *The Philosophy of Marsilio Ficino*; E. Law, *Shakespeare's 'Tempest' as Produced at Court*; J. H. Long, *Shakespeare's Use of Music: Final Comedies*; A. Nicoll, *Stuart Masques and the Renaissance Stage*; E. C. Pettet, *Shakespeare and the Romance Tradition*; E. M. W. Tillyard, *Shakespeare's Last Plays*; D. P. Walker, *Spiritual and Demonic Magic from Ficino to Campanella*; E. Welsford, *The Court Masque*; R. H. West, *The Invisible World*.

I acknowledge too with gratitude the stimulation and information received from articles by the following: J. Cutts, J. Davidson, Margaret Hogden, W. Stacy Johnson, J. M. Nosworthy, J. E. Phillips, J. Robinson, Rose Zimbardo.

J.H.W.

INTRODUCTION

I

FIRST PERFORMANCES

AN entry in the *Revels Accounts* for 1 November, 1611, is the first record of a performance of *The Tempest*: 'By the King's Players: Hallowmas nyght was presented att Whithall before ye Kinges Maiestie, a play called the Tempest'.

At a royal command performance such as this it was customary to present King James with a programme in the form of an illuminated 'table', or synopsis of the plot and the words of any songs. As a pleasant fancy, we may enlarge this programme with details in modern style: 'Scenery and sets designed by Inigo Jones. Incidental music composed by Antonio Ferrabosco, and played by His Majesty's Consort of Musicians. Songs arranged by Robert Johnson for lute accompaniment.'

The play was staged in the Banqueting Hall which was specially constructed for the production of plays and masques. It was a hall some 170 feet by 60 feet with at one end a stage 40 feet square divided into upper (rear) and lower levels. It had an arch somewhat similar to the modern proscenium. The walls of the auditorium had galleries for spectators, and in the centre of the floor space was the king's throne on a dais, on either side of which were stools for those of the highest rank.

Elaborate structures and mechanical devices were available for the simulation of moving clouds, flowing waves, and descending gods. There were traverse curtains, backcloths painted with vistas or seascapes, lighting effects by candelabra, a 'music house' draped with silk to conceal the orchestra, and possibly three-sided 'flats' to facilitate scene-changing. In addition there were stores of properties: rocks, trees, caves, banks, arbours, etc. Costumes were rich and splendid. Those worn by Ariel and the spirits in their

3

various guises symbolized the nature and powers of the character they represented.

The Venetian ambassador was astounded at the opulence and magnificence of the audience, resplendent with costly garments and jewellery, that attended the entertainments at this time: 'The King's own cloak, breeches and jacket were all sewn with diamonds, a rope and jewel of diamonds also in his hat of inestimable value. . . .' The Queen 'had in her hair a very great number of pear-shaped pearls, the largest and most beautiful in the world; and there were diamonds all over her person, so that she was ablaze'.

Was this the 'first night' of *The Tempest*? Editors and commentators tend to think that the play had been performed previously at the Globe or at the Blackfriars Theatre. There is no direct evidence either way. The play was certainly written after about October 1610 when reports of the shipwreck of the *Sea-Adventure* reached England. Indeed, if Shakespeare did take the word 'wallets' from Boemus, *The Manners, Laws and Customs of All Nations*, 1611, and not from Ortelius, *The Theatre of the Whole World*, 1606, the play must have been written after 25 March, 1611, i.e. after the beginning of the year old style. (See Appendix I.) In which case this royal performance may well have been its première.

Just over a year later in February 1613 it was again produced at Court as one of the numerous entertainments at the festivities celebrating the marriage of Princess Elizabeth to the Elector Palatine.

II

THE NATURE OF THE PLAY

The numerous attempts to formulate the aim of *The Tempest*, or simply to account for its content, indicate not only the varying dimensions of interpretation, but also the disintegration of its unity. It has been described as—a return to the romance types of

4

his early period; an early play reshaped; an imitation of the plays of Beaumont and Fletcher; autobiographical; a version of the much debated topic 'Nature versus Art'; a discussion on colonization; a sermon on the christian virtue of forgiveness after repentance; a working out of the themes of reconciliation and regeneration; a portrayal of the relations between the three parts (rational, sensitive, vegetative) of the soul; a parable on order and disorder throughout the universe; a 'complicated masque or narrative poem with lyrical intervals'; purgatorial and elysian; a dream; a 'metaphor of metamorphosis'; a 'mirror of Creation in human terms, with love shaping a new world out of chaos to the sound of music'; a play on the Redemption.

There is general agreement, however, that it is a fairy story, not of the folk-tale or of the pantomime kind although it has two wicked uncles, a magician who spell-binds a handsome prince, a fairy, and an evil beast, but of the kind called romances, which were devised to entertain a leisured, courtly audience, but which were very popular among all classes in Shakespeare's time. Romances were tales set vaguely in some past time of how young noble or royal lovers suffered hardships, separations, misunderstandings, shipwrecks, treachery, false imprisonments in a world of fantasy, of marvels and wonders and magic, inhabited by villainous nobles, giants, ogres, necromancers, shepherds, pirates, fair damsels, enchanters, witches, and how, after many years wandering, amid surprises and suspense, lost children are restored to their parents, the wicked punished or killed, and 'journeys end in lovers' meeting'. Their aim was to entertain and to delight, and, at the same time to instruct, to encourage the nobly born to 'vertuous and gentle discipline' whereby they might be moved to the 'exercise of courtesy, liberality and especially courage'. The romances reaffirm the validity of a given social, usually chivalric order, they are a means of self identification with magnanimity, and hence by their very fantastic unreality liberate and enhance the human spirit.

Although *The Tempest* contains many romance features, and one can take pleasure in it simply as a romantic story, yet its differences from the general romance type are considerable and profound. Foremost in importance among the differences are the nature of Prospero's magic, his position as magician-ruler, Ariel's quality and musical activities, and certain aspects of the treatment of time and change. Prospero's magic and Ariel's existence among other things are not just Shakespeare's flights of fanciful invention, they are precisely and consistently grounded in a version of a philosophical theory of the universe which had many adherents in England, in other words they were rationally demonstrable and acceptable realities. Prospero performs his magic feats in person, through the 'airy spirit' Ariel, through Ariel's music and song, and through background song and instrumental music. His magic is essentially white magic free from trafficking with Satan, it is never used merely to amuse or for frivolous entertainment, and it is more extensive and elevated than the magic of other contemporary play-magicians. Its virtuous and benevolent nature is firmly stressed, for a very commonly held rival theory maintained that all magicians were in league with Satan, and that the spirits they commanded were evil spirits.

Philosophies generally were agreed that all created things were arranged in orderly degrees and made complementary in function by God. There were detailed analogies between the physical heavens (the macrocosm) and man (the microcosm), similarly between both these and the political state. Thus disorders in one corresponded to disorders in the others. In *Julius Cæsar*, storms in the heavens correspond to the perturbation in Brutus' mind and to the political assassination of Cæsar. Celestial influences from the sun and the planets were constantly pouring on human beings. The particular philosophy that informs and illuminates *The Tempest* is a version of neo-platonism, so called because it was derived from a renewed study of Plato, Pythagoras, and their followers. Here the references are taken mainly from Cornelius

Agrippa's *Occult Philosophy*, a most popular book throughout the sixteenth and seventeenth centuries. It described all creation as threefold: elementary, the elements as studied in natural philosophy; celestial, the heavenly bodies as studied in astrology and mathematics; intellectual, religion, as studied in theology, and ceremonial magic. Corresponding with these were the three parts of the soul: vegetative, concerned with nourishment, growth, and reproduction; sensitive, concerned with knowledge through the senses, imagination, memory, movement; rational, concerned with reason, judgment, and will. These correspondences were likewise extended to involve the civil state (the slaves and peasants, the officers of the realm, and the king) and man's body (the digestive organs, the heart, and the head).

In such a universe it was held to be confirmed by 'the famousest philosophers and theologians' that men with 'pure divine minds, inflamed with religious love . . . directed by faith . . . elevated by these theological vertues' could 'command the elements, drive away fogs, raise the winds, cause rain, cure diseases, raise the dead', and see into the future. Yet the power of religion by itself would not suffice, unless a man 'be made totally intellectual', in which case he would not live long but would merge into the divine intelligence. Astrological observations to gain the help of celestial influences and spirits, and knowledgeable use of the properties of natural objects were necessary preliminaries to magical practice. All these were the fruits of prolonged study. Above everything the magus or magician must have absolute purity of mind in order to invoke celestial influences. He must abstain from all 'affections, imaginations, opinions, and such like passions, which hurt the mind and pervert the judgment of reasons, as we manifestly see in the lascivious, the envious, and ambitious passions'.

The magus sought the help of a high ranking, powerful good spirit who compelled evil or inferior spirits to do his bidding. Spirits were composed of air or fire and often had a luminous appearance like a will-o'-the-wisp or St Elmo's fire. They were organized in hierarchies and inhabited the heavenly spheres. They could transmit celestial influences to other creatures, and, as their substance was airy, like the vital spirits in man, they could act on a man's spirit and soul. Ariel, as Prospero reminds us, was 'but air', and air in the same theory 'is a vital spirit, passing through all beings . . . a medium or glue joining all things together, and . . . the resounding spirit of the world's instrument'. It immediately receives into itself the influences of all celestial bodies, and then communicates them to the other elements. It retains as if it were a divine looking glass the species of all things and all manner of speeches, and carries them into the bodies of men both when they are asleep to cause dreams, and when they are awake. Naturally therefore Ariel is in affinity with music. Music which was carried by air directly into a man's ear and so was intermingled with his vital spirits, therefore, had a more powerful influence than anything communicated by the other senses. As the universe was created in harmony and maintained in musical tones and movements, music was apt to receive heavenly influences. Thus it accompanied any manifestation of divinity. Singing in particular even more than instrumental music could transfer the thought, imagination, emotion of the singer, evil or bad, into the mind of the listener, 'moreover it moveth and stoppeth the members and the humours of the body'. It could compel 'both singer and hearer to imitate and perform the same things'.

Prospero the magician-ruler is unusual. Shakespeare was always very much concerned with rule and kingship, and it seems to have escaped notice how insistent is the theme of rule or government in this play. Apart from Prospero, seven characters have an interest in ruling, and the kinds of society they would establish are clearly shown. Caliban, originally his 'own king' of a state established by evil, inspires Stephano to seek to murder Prospero and establish a rule of drunkenness and lust. Antonio attempts to proliferate his machiavellian evil by urging Sebastian to commit murder and usurp the crown of Naples. Gonzalo proposes, challengingly or whimsically, an unregulated golden age containing its own contradiction. Ferdinand, the lawful heir to the throne of Naples, regrets that his father's presumed death makes him king, but undergoes discipline that reveals his integrity and willingness for service. His father Alonso surrenders himself to grief and despair, and rejecting Gonzalo's counsel abdicates his authority.

Prospero, it is important to notice, failed twice as a ruler: he allowed corruption to destroy his rule in Milan, and on the island early sympathy for Caliban and failure to keep him in subjection nearly ended in the disastrous multiplication of evil. Having learnt from experience and thus demonstrating to the audience that 'degree' must be maintained, Prospero accepts that a ruler must be vigilant and use compulsion. His kingdom on the island is a model of rule, it is the civil state stripped of its social trappings and reduced to a single representative for each of the three estates. Caliban represents the slave labourers, Ariel the officers of the state, and Prospero the ruler. Furthermore the correspondences hold: Caliban is of the earth, elementary, Ariel is of the air, celestial, Prospero is of the soul, intellectual; again, Caliban represents the vegetative part (some have even alleged that Caliban and Ariel stand for the vegetative and sensitive parts of Prospero's soul) Ariel the sensitive, and Prospero the rational. Both Caliban and Ariel are handled firmly almost harshly and made aware of their obligations to Prospero. As in the universe, music and harmony regulate and maintain Prospero's rule.

The constant references to time in the play led Traversi to observe 'in the total context of its conflict, poetry and themes— time is the central element of the form and meaning of the play'. Valuable though this judgment is it is incomplete; it is Providence working through time that determines the significance of events and, in the human condition, their end. Time by itself is uncommitted, it is 'tutor both to good and bad' (*Lucrece*, 995).

9

Prospero, preserved by Providence (I. ii, 159) in terms of the above philosophy was admitted by his celestial studies to the 'secret disposition of God's providence'. He is not Providence, but the agent of Providence, just as a king is God's representative, and so is aware of mutability, of time passing. The 'auspicious star' passes swiftly through the celestial house, 'bountiful Fortune' on her rolling sphere changes rapidly, and magical operations, like alchemical projection (V. i, 1–2) are subject to a crisis of efficacy. The would-be rulers and evil doers too, are anxious to seize their opportunity, believing that Fortune is favouring them. Prospero presents in a vision of judgment the end for the wicked, and after a vision of blessing for the virtuous rulers-elect, reminds them of the providential limitation of human affairs. Providence through time makes it 'Time's glory' not only 'to bring truth to light', 'to wrong the wronger till he render right', but also to 'ruinate proud buildings . . . And smear with dust their glitt'ring golden tow'rs . . . To feed oblivion with decay of things' (*Lucrece*, 939–947). In his revels speech Prospero, the agent of Providence, confirms the temporality of human existence.

Prospero is then as a ruler the representative of Providence, and the philosopher-magician. Within his kingdom in essence old wrongs are righted, and the rightness of the providential ordering of human societies is made manifest. Prospero himself proposes to meditate on death. His studies and magic are discarded. He has attained virtue and serenity of mind 'all passion spent', and may now contemplate the ascent to the divine intelligence which was the ultimate stage of platonic philosophers.

In brief the play is a brilliant, exciting exposition of rule within the topical neo-platonic metaphysical theory, it is a mirror of society controlled by a philosopher-king. In giving the play a kind of all embracing time, which comprehends past time, suggests present time, and reflects on future time, Shakespeare gave it a universality and immediacy that related it to the rule of James I. Whether James, who subscribed in his *Demonology 1597* to the opposing view that magicians were workers in evil, saw something of himself in Prospero and sanctioned a repeat performance of the play as a profitable entertainment at the wedding festivities of the Elector Palatine and Princess Elizabeth is an attractive speculation that must be left unresolved. But it is nevertheless of interest that some four years earlier he had been honoured with the title Rex Platonicus.

III

THEMES

The Tempest has a number of themes in common with Shakespeare's other romances: reconciliation, forgiveness, regeneration, nature versus art, children lost and found, and it is perhaps sufficient merely to mention these. Nowhere else in his plays is the theme of metamorphosis so widely and beautifully expressed. Metamorphosis of a violent and disconcerting kind was associated with the traditional magician, and Caliban indeed feared transformation of himself and his companions into 'barnacles or apes with foreheads villainous low'. But Prospero's magic does not degrade men, its purpose is to restore and exalt them, to increase their knowledge of self, and to raise them as it were on the scale of perfection in terms of neo-platonism. Thus the changes he brings about are always ultimately from disorder to order and storm to calm in the heavens and in the minds of men, ignorance turns to self-knowledge, and evil to good. Ariel's beautiful song, 'Full fathom five', in which corrupt mortality suffers a 'sea change into something rich and strange' is not only a delightful dramatic device it is also an exquisite statement of the themes. Ariel himself has been called a symbol of change. It is hinted at in the imagery of clouds dissolving and melting, of reason that had ebbed flooding back, and in changes of state between sleeping and waking. Prospero describes the dissolution from dream-life to sleep that sets a period to man's endeavour;

Gonzalo welcomes the change whereby each one has attained self-knowledge; and Miranda exhilarated and in love sees a 'brave new world', a new regenerate society. In Prospero's kingdom men come to a knowledge of themselves and fulfil themselves within the divinely appointed order.

The part played by music in Prospero's magic has been mentioned above. Nowhere else does Shakespeare display so full an awareness of the neo-platonic conception of its powers nor employ it as so comprehensive and integral a part of the play. It is as if all the characters are enmeshed in a web of music and song contrived by Prospero through Ariel.

The musical calming of the storm is symbolized by the ordered dance of the sprites in Ariel's first song. Ariel's music leads Ferdinand to Prospero's cell, and his song 'Full fathom five' announces the theme of metamorphosis which pervades the whole play. Convinced that the music is 'no mortal business' Ferdinand invests Miranda in greater wonder as 'the goddess On whom these airs attend'. Later in the same scene Ariel plays solemn music, which lulls to sleep all the company except Antonio and Sebastian who, presumably because they are 'fit for treasons, stratagems and spoils', have no music in their souls. This is a further condemnation of the characters already established as cynical and scoffing. The scurvy tunes and song of Stephano, no doubt learnt from the more ribald among the sailors, and the drunken howling and hiccoughing of Caliban introduce discord and disorder with the touch of lechery. Later their failure to remember a tune and Ariel's sudden playing of the correct tune on a pipe and tabor frighten Stephano and Trinculo but not Caliban, who beast-like has found his glimpse of paradise in the island's music. Reassured they follow Ariel's music into the 'filthy-mantled pool'.

Solemn music introduces the shapes bringing the banquet and accompanies their mimetic dancing, and music underlines their derisory gestures as they remove the table. Action and music render Alonso, Sebastian, and Antonio distraught. Alonso becomes suddenly aware that the angry music of the storm noise denounces him for the enormity of his crime against Prospero.

The harmony, order, and blessing devised in the masque are symbolized together with chastity and fruitfulness in the 'graceful dance' of the reapers and nymphs. The approach of Caliban and his conspirators, rudely shatters the harmony into a 'confused noise'. Solemn, heavenly music draws Alonso and his courtiers to Prospero's cell and slowly restores their distracted minds to calm and sanity. Cutting across the solemnity comes Ariel's joyous lyric of freedom. It heralds the change not only of his own state, but the freedom of the others from Prospero's spell and from the slavery of their own sinful passions.

Another theme is the movement of the sea. The pulse of the sea beats throughout from the 'wild waters in this roar' of the opening to the 'calm seas and auspicious gales' that waft all but Ariel, and presumably Caliban, back to Naples and Milan. There are spirits that disport themselves in the ebb and flow of the sea. The images of ebbing and flowing tides, and of beating seas recur. Antonio turns the ebb-tide of Sebastian's fortunes to the flood of conspiracy, Prospero's solemn music brings reason flooding back to the minds of the courtiers whence it had ebbed. Ferdinand's grief for his father was 'never since at ebb'. Miranda, Prospero and Alonso all at one time or another have uneasy minds that echo the beating of the sea. Always there seems to be a threatening undertone of storm and passion until the tide of reason returns and calm seas are restored.

There are an unusual number of words in which 'sea' is combined with another word: 'sea-storm', 'sea-change', 'sea-nymph', 'sea-sorrow', 'sea-swallowed', 'sea-side', 'sea-water'. Apart from the many direct references to the initial tempest, there are other references to the sea: Prospero's voyage (I. ii, 144–55), Ariel's activities (I. ii, 252–3), and his songs (I. ii, 375, 395), islands (II. i, 86). Alonso thinks of drowning himself 'deeper than e'er

plummet sounded', and Prospero in echoing words undertakes
to drown his book.

Sleep is imminent all through the play. Miranda sleeps while
Prospero reprimands Ariel. Alonso and his followers are put to
sleep by Ariel's music. Antonio and Sebastian broach their conspiracy in terms of the image of sleep; Caliban is ecstatic over the
dreams that sleep brings, the mariners are put to sleep; Prospero
reflects on the sleep of death that rounds off the dream that is life.
There are changes of states between sleeping and waking,
illusion and reality, transitions that are induced or accompanied
by music and song. Words and images of melting, dissolving,
vanishing also assist the fluidity of states of being.

IV

PROSPERO

In creating Prospero Shakespeare may have taken a hint from
Ben Jonson's masques, the main purpose of which was to display
the beneficient, just rule of James I as the ideal monarch. Passages
in his masques 'suggest a world centring on the office of a
monarchy, which is itself patterned on a universal philosophy'.
Prospero's actions are similarly held up for approval. He is not
only the chief actor in the play he is also a kind of Presenter or
chorus; he not only explains and justifies his motives to the
audience, but also indicates to them the moral values to be set on
the actions and motives of others. Throughout the play Prospero
is by the spectator's side pointing out, commenting, directing,
judging, explaining; indeed he rarely leaves the stage without
telling the audience what he is going to do next. Even when in
silence he watches the other characters from above, his presence
may perhaps have reminded audiences of the woodcuts in which
God was depicted overseeing the world, and communicated to
them some feeling of his powerful influence.

This supremacy of Prospero has led some to define him as—

superman, God, poet with Ariel as his imagination, priest, rational soul, symbol of art or nurture, epitome of Shakespeare's tragic heroes.

Shakespeare took care to emphasize Prospero's integrity among other things lest his magic should be suspect. Its effects are always accounted 'strange' never 'unnatural' a word with sinister implications of black magic and witchcraft. The tempest, Miranda and the audience are assured, has harmed no-one on the ship, indeed it is wholly for Miranda's benefit. His magic too was used to break the evil spell by which Sycorax imprisoned Ariel. His renunciation of his magical powers is carried out with impressive ceremony. To suggest, as some have done that his claim to have opened graves and raised the dead strikes a false note, and is carried over from the source of the speech will not bear examination. It was one of the established and legitimate powers of the white magician. If the members of the audience recognized the speech as coming from Medea's invocation when about to renew Æson's youth, they may well have understood that for Prospero there was to be no evil magic and no renewal of youth. His insistence on chastity is also demanded by his practice of magic; magic under Providence demanded the utmost purity and abstinence in the magus and in the end for which it was employed.

Though Ferdinand approves of Prospero, 'so rare a wondered father and a wise', some of Prospero's human traits are thought to diminish his stature. As a ruler he confessedly neglected his duties, became too much the 'contemplative man', and, lacking the vigilance of a good ruler, gave his brother the opportunity to usurp the state. He treats Ariel with severity and Caliban with harshness. He is a man of strong passions. On his banishment he gave way to despair until Miranda's innocence brought him fortitude. He is impatient with Miranda, irritable at times, forgetful, prone to righteous indignation, kindly, given to moralizing or uttering sententious asides. Yet these touches of mere humanity are important. For Prospero as an abstraction or as a symbol the forgiving of his enemies would be meaningless; it is only by an earthly ruler and within human terms that 'the rarer action Is in virtue than in vengeance' becomes meaningful.

V

ARIEL

Ariel, an airy spirit, as the Folio character-list describes him, is clearly derived from the neo-platonic hierarchy of spirits and demons, though he is not the earth-spirit of that name. The name had been used in stories of magic and in the *Bible*, but Shakespeare displays no knowledge of this. As air, Ariel's association with music is readily deducible from the qualities and affinities assigned to both in the same philosophy. He has moreover the qualities and capacities of air for movement as rapid as thought, pervasion of elements including the 'veins of the earth', instant apprehension of influences, speech, and happenings. Accordingly he acts as Prospero's intelligencer and messenger, and as such is the main-spring of much of the action.

On the other hand he has the playfulness of Puck in leading Stephano, Trinculo, and Caliban into the pond, and in releasing the sailors. In his relationship with Prospero he resembles the familiar spirit of the traditional magician. Indeed he may have appeared on stage in the likeness of a bird, for Prospero addresses him as 'my bird' and 'chick'. His appearances as classical figures, a sea-nymph, a harpy, and either Iris or Ceres are in keeping with conventional treatment of the divinities, particularly in masques. He has been variously described as the personification of poetry, Prospero's imagination, and the sensitive soul.

VI

MIRANDA

Miranda is a slight figure beside the women in Shakespeare's comedies, but she is by no means insignificant. Had her characterization been ampler and deeper it would have detracted from the dominance of Prospero, and it is clear that Shakespeare intended Prospero's activities to be the main interest of the play.

As her name suggests she attracts wonder and admiration from Caliban as well as Ferdinand, she herself has the capacity for wonder. Her wonder at Ferdinand and at the 'brave new world' is spontaneous and sincere. Some regard her as a symbol of fertility, others as original virtue, chastity, love, or beauty. Yet the quality that stands out is her pity. Her first speech and her tears reveal her sympathy for the ship's company as she presses Prospero to calm the storm. Again she weeps at the tale of Prospero's misfortunes, and for pity at Ferdinand's humiliating labours. The readiness with which she champions the cause of the voyagers on the ship, and springs to the defence of Ferdinand makes her forthright denunciation of Caliban the more surprising, but it should serve to impress on the audience Caliban's animal nature. Elsewhere she sees only good in mankind, and is generous and impulsive in her actions. She surprises Prospero by her sudden spirited opposition: 'What, my foot my tutor!' Later she meets Ferdinand, assuming that Prospero was 'safe for these three hours', and disobeys him by revealing her name to Ferdinand. Her love at first sight is part of the platonic love convention, as is her belief that Ferdinand is a spirit, and that his manly beauty witnesses to a virtuous nature: 'there's nothing ill can dwell in such a temple.'

She has the frankness of some of the ballad maidens: 'I am your wife if you will marry me; If not I'll die your maid'. Sometimes her frankness is disconcerting: 'by my modesty, The jewel in my dower', but it is in keeping with the theme of order that prevails throughout the play. Her noble birth is pointedly made clear by Prospero's elaborate statement, 'Thy mother was a piece of virtue . . . issued', and similarly her education has been more thorough than that usually given to princesses. Both by birth and breeding therefore is she above question, for by innate disposition and careful nurture she is virtuous and nobly given.

Ferdinand's tribute to Miranda: 'The mistress which I serve quickens what's dead' carries more significance than he realized. Not only did she bring new life to him, but the 'heaven that lay about' her infancy infused a new life and purpose in her despairing father.

Her last words in the play wonderfully reflect her nature. Her 'brave new world' has been thought to carry overtones of irony since it refers to a usurper and two would-be murderers, but they have been changed by repentance to a state of grace.

The words spoken from an innocent heart enshrine as in a crystal the meaning of the play. She sees only the beauty of a divinely ordered human society, formerly corrupt, but now informed and transfigured by the virtue of Prospero's island. The civil state, and not 'world nature' however paradisal, is ordained for mankind.

VII

FERDINAND

Ferdinand too is lightly sketched. He has the attributes of the conventional courtly lover (in the platonic mode). For him Miranda is composed of every creature's best, his slavery is endurable because of her presence, he professes with extravagant vows his love for her. It has been held that he is curiously lacking in rapture when he expresses a hope for 'quiet days, fair issue, and long life', but his thought implies stability of mind rather than volatility of emotion. As legitimate heir and king-elect to the throne of Naples this together with the ideal of service he has learnt are eminently apt qualities.

VIII

ANTONIO AND SEBASTIAN

Antonio and Sebastian are breakers of order and harmony. Antonio's hectoring request for the Master to the prejudice of the orderly carrying out of the Boatswain's work is characteristic. They blame others for the predicament in which they find themselves. They curse the crew to whose inefficiency and drunkenness they attribute the loss of the ship and possibly their lives; they blame Alonso for marrying his daughter to an African, and for that reason undertaking the voyage. His hostile, destructive criticism indicative of disaffection is the springboard from which Antonio's treacheries are projected. Thus all Gonzalo's attempts to console Alonso, to encourage him to see things in proportion, to rouse him from the apathy of despair, and to assume his authority are thwarted by the cynical jeering and contradictions with which they 'darken counsel'. They side with lechery in talking of Dido, and the unicorn and phœnix, symbols of chastity, Sebastian had considered beyond belief. Their strained wit is directed at making a butt of the king's adviser.

Once the others are asleep, Antonio's flippancy hardens into policy of the machiavellian type. He is an opportunist unable to refrain from practising evil for its own sake. The brilliance of his seduction of Sebastian has touches of the master villain Iago about it, and some parallels with Macbeth have been noted. He ingeniously develops Sebastian's comment on sleep and waking to suggest that it is Sebastian's fortune that sleeps, that he is not awake to his opportunity. He further seizes Sebastian's non-committal 'standing water' and 'hereditary sloth' to show that Sebastian is more concerned about his inferiority in rank than he openly admits. Having stimulated Sebastian to hope from the 'no hope' of Ferdinand's survival he then applies more pressure. The claims of Claribel are dismissed with contemptuous iteration, Sebastian's understatement 'some space' is enlarged to prove Antonio's case. Sebastian's demur about his conscience he sweeps aside atheistically with the derisive images of a chilblain and a dissolving sweetmeat.

Prospero apparently forgives their conspiracy more lightly than he does the parallel conspiracy of Caliban. Neither of them utters a word of regret or repentance. Perhaps it should be assumed that the vision of judgment and their subsequent frantic behaviour had brought them to a state of acceptance. In any case they have recovered in time to laugh at Caliban. Is this meant to indicate a wholesome attitude, or are we to consider Antonio unregenerate? W. H. Auden's words,

> I am I Antonio,
> My choice myself Alone

seem more applicable to, say Richard III, than to Antonio, whose gratuitous treachery would by murder seek to place not himself but Sebastian on a throne he may never see.

IX

GONZALO

Gonzalo preserves a degree of calmness and balance amid the storm at sea and the vexed passions of his companions. On board ship he even contemplates the approach of death with a glimpse of wry humour. He is resourceful but unsuccessful in his attempts to console and rouse Alonso, and to fend from him the malicious accusations of Antonio and Sebastian. Antonio's gibe 'What impossible matter will he make easy next?' contains an element of truth, it was indeed one aspect of Gonzalo's work.

He has a courteous appreciation of the spirits who bring the banquet, not like Antonio and Sebastian, a bad mannered wonder at their shapes. He encourages others to restrain Alonso, Sebastian, and Antonio from 'what their ecstasy may provoke them to'. He is a preserver of society. Prospero's words 'my true preserver, and loyal sir To him thou follow'st' sum up his integrity.

True to his nature he places the events of the play in perspective when, calling down a blessing and a crown on Ferdinand and Miranda, he sums up the bountiful fortune of the voyage in

which Claribel found a husband, Ferdinand a wife, Prospero his
dukedom and all of them found themselves,

When no man was his own.

X

CALIBAN

Like Prospero Caliban has been variously interpreted: an
earth-spirit in contrast to Ariel, a projection of the animal nature
of Prospero himself, a symbol of the vegetative soul in man, a
'woodwose' or wild man common in pageants, spectacles, and
illustrations from the middle ages onwards, a native of the West
Indies as reported by sailors, the deformed offspring of a witch
and a devil and hence a symbol of evil and chaos. Some of these
are partial views. If the play is a mirror of governance, a demon-
stration of rule, then in the Elizabethan pattern of analogical
thinking as between the civil state, the constitution of man, and
the cosmic order, Caliban could represent more than one of the
above views. His description in the original character list, 'a
salvage and deformed slave' and his mother Sycorax link him
with both the natives of the new world and the witchcraft of the
old world. By birth he is of 'vile race' and has not inherited that
'seed of virtue in the soul' which makes him capable of courtly
and civilized manners. Accordingly all attempts to educate him
fail because although he has learned language, responds to music,
and dreams of riches he has no rational control over his emotions.
Rape, murder, and worship of a drunkard come naturally to him;
physical pain and pleasure coupled with a desire for revenge are
his only motivations.

Prospero's epithets for him ring harshly: 'poisonous slave',
'lying slave', 'hag-seed', 'malice', 'filth', 'thing of darkness',
'demi-devil'. Even Miranda considers him an 'abhorred slave'
and finds his appearance repulsive, a reflection of the evil nature

within. Stephano and Trinculo find him a fairground freak, as do Antonio and Sebastian. It is characteristic of him that he inspires Stephano to attempt murder, that he like an evil Vice is their guide and instructor.

Yet some human elements in him aroused at first Miranda's pity to which he responded with devotion. He represents Prospero's rule, and if he is regarded as an innocent native, it is possible to sympathize with his claim that he has been dispossessed of the island by Prospero. In view of his origin, however, this is not tenable, Prospero's assumption of rule is the triumph of good over evil.

Perhaps it may not be far-fetched to suggest that after his muddy baptism in the filthy-mantled pool and the driving out of his passions by the spirit-hounds even to him came some degree of self-knowledge and the possibility of redemption. He admits his folly, admires Prospero above the other 'brave spirits' of the court, intends to be wise in the future and, in words which may well carry overtones of meaning decides to, 'seek for grace' rather than take a 'drunkard for a god'.

XI

IMAGES, DEVICES OF STYLE, WORDS

In keeping with the theme of metamorphosis many images indicate change particularly the dissolving and vanishing of clouds, the ebbing of the sea, the coming of dawn. Caroline Spurgeon states that images of sound predominate, that the isle is indeed 'full of noises'. Clemen points out the numerous images and words relating to animal and vegetable life, some of it hostile in tone to the treacherous characters, a not surprising state of affairs since Ariel warns the court party, 'The powers . . . have Incensed the seas and shores, yea all the creatures Against your peace'. Perhaps the audience is intended to note that the winds that pitied Prospero and Miranda on the other hand drove

Alonso ashore, and that Antonio and Sebastian see only an eye of green in tawny grass, foul air, and barrenness where Gonzalo and Adrian find fruitfulness, soft air, and lush and lusty growth.

The images of *The Tempest* have not the intense fusing and astonishing associative leaps that characterize the images in Shakespeare's tragedies. The 'rough magic' imagery of the latter, born of stormy involved passions, has become in the former elegant grace in a world of self-controlled or externally directed emotions. Some of the major characters appear to be detached from complete identification with their feelings. Prospero recounts the perfidy of his brother with interspersed comments of moral judgment. Not until Miranda apologizes for the trouble she caused him does he admit to a personal grief which Miranda's presence encouraged him to endure. Ferdinand woos Miranda within a prescribed platonic convention which overlays his feelings. Small wonder is it that Miranda prompted by 'plain and holy innocence' finds it necessary to ask him to marry her. Antonio and Sebastian are very superficial, and in their distracted state they are spell-bound.

From a rhetorical view Prospero's speeches are most skilfully constructed: the presentation is varied, points made are reinforced by a proverb or crystallized in an apt image, or amplified by illustration. He takes the terms, 'foul play . . . thence . . . blessed' (I. ii, 60–1), used by Miranda and deftly extends them into an alliterative antithesis, 'foul play . . . heaved thence . . . blessedly holp hither' (I. ii, 62–3). Some of his images that condense thought are memorable: 'subject his coronet to his crown' (I. ii, 114), and the famous 'We are such stuff As dreams are made on' (IV. i, 156–7). At times he speaks with ritual tones, 'The fringed curtains of thine eye advance' (I. ii, 407). A similar weighty phrase, 'the dark backward and abysm of time' (I. ii, 50) is perhaps intended to divorce the past from the present by emphasizing its remoteness. Again the 'Thy mother was a piece of virtue, and She said thou wast my daughter' (I. ii, 56–7) far from being facetious bad taste, is intended to make very clear to the audience as necessary to the plot, Miranda's nobility of birth. For the most part his images are not sustained though 'Not a frown further' (V. i, 30) refers back to 'fury' four lines before, and 'rankest' (V. i, 132) may be an echo of 'infect' (l, 131). In one speech (I. ii, 79–87) there is a string of impressive images ranging from the checking of hounds to the clinging of ivy while the meaning of one image shifts from key (lock) to key (music). A few of his images may be related to emblems bearing traditional symbols, and it may be that Shakespeare was thus adding overtones to an apparently simple image. Thus the 'ivy' image (I. ii, 86–7) is complex. The ivy obscures not only Prospero but also his rightful descent ('princely trunk'), and parasitically weakens his position by its ambitious greed. Ivy was usurping (*Comedy of Errors*, II. ii, 180) and it was an adornment of the emblem of ambition. The emblem of authority has both keys and books among its symbols, and it will be remembered that Antonio obtained the 'key to officer and office', but for Prospero his 'library Was dukedom enough'. Elsewhere in the play there may be similar links with the emblems of conspiracy ('open-eyed conspiracy', II. i, 292), ambition ('crown Dropping upon thy head', II. i, 199–200), and chastity ((Cupid) 'has broke his arrows', IV. i, 99). This possible relationship with emblems needs further examination than it is possible to give it here. At another level Prospero is capable of some alliterative imperatives, 'Hag seed hence fetch us in fuel', perhaps as a counter to Caliban's alliterative cursing, 'blow on you and blister you all o'er'.

Antonio and Sebastian are noteworthy for their abasing or deflating similes and their strained quibbling and punning. It is not sufficient to note that the similes and comparisons involve simple domestic things, they indicate the contempt felt by the speaker for the person or topic under discussion and with economy and decorum betray his cynical character. Such are 'like cold porridge' (II. i, 10), 'as a cat laps milk' (II. i, 279), 'tell the clock' (II. i, 280), 'if 'twere a kibe, 'Twould put me to my slipper' (II. i, 267–8). With cheap, superficial mockery and scorn they attempt to defeat Gonzalo's efforts to bring comfort and self-control to Alonso. They disparage Alonso, who, they allege, is responsible for their shipwreck; Antonio belittles Gonzalo as a mere spirit of persuasion; and sweeps aside the others as completely subservient. His speech that dismisses Claribel's claim to the throne (II. i, 237–45) with its contemptuous repetition, 'She that . . .', its derisory inflated images, and its hinted intention in sustained theatrical images is most ingeniously devised. Antonio's climactic speech in which he persuades Sebastian to murder is a masterpiece of images swift changing in tone, cynical, hypocritical, earnest, and scornful.

The puns, quibbles, and direct denials with which Antonio and Sebastian deride Gonzalo have perplexed many, and have given rise to comments like boring, tedious, and accusations that Shakespeare was faltering. Yet in their dramatic context their value is more apparent. Antonio in particular is a villain, presumably known to be a villain from Prospero's account in I. ii, although it is not mentioned directly until II. i, 261–2 (Sebastian is mentioned a little earlier, II. i, 131). He does not, like Don John in *Much Ado* and other Vice-like villains, declare his villainy to the audience, it is unfolded in his speech and his actions. So the strained, trivial, and malicious sallies he makes at Gonzalo's expense establish convincingly the man he is, they are not intended to enlist the approval of the audience by brilliant repartee and delightful humour, but to emphasize the negative barren philosophy of the machiavellian man.

Trinculo is not one of Shakespeare's memorable jesters; some would even deny him that title. His wit is mainly confined to commonplace puns and quibbles: 'set' (III. ii, 8); 'standard' (III. ii, 15); monster (i.e. unnatural) = natural (III. ii, 29–30); pickle (V. i, 282); and he rises to the heights in 'line and level' (IV. i, 237). He has little trace of the loquacious, irrepressible cheerfulness of Lancelot Gobbo or the intelligence of Touchstone. His partner Stephano rarely attempts a pun, but his delight over the discovery of the 'glistering apparel' burst forth in a quibble on 'line' (IV. i, 233–5) accompanied by stage business. Ferdinand's 'Admired Miranda' is a courteous compliment, but Caliban's 'red plague rid you' is a curse. It is possible that Gonzalo's 'dry death' is perhaps something of a dry jest. Prospero is not normally considered as punning, but there may be a jingle of sounds not too far apart in 'pine' (I. ii, 277) and 'painfully' (I. ii, 278), and rather more convincingly in 'oaths are straw' (IV. i, 52), where 'th' in 'oaths' may have been pronounced as 't'. (See *Henry V*, II. iii, 51 for this phrase, and compare the pun on 'Goths' and 'goats' in *As You Like It*, III. iii, 5, 6.)

While it is not unusual to find words or phrases repeated in a play of Shakespeare, occasionally the iteration is significant. Thus the sense of mystery that pervades the play is aided by the repetition of 'strange' and its derivates on eighteen occasions, and by 'wonder' and its derivates on ten occasions. Links are sometimes suggested between characters or events which while establishing a similarity may also mark a difference. 'Delicate' is thrice applied to Ariel, twice—once with a quibble—to temperance, and once extraordinarily to Caliban. Both Sebastian and Caliban suffer 'pinches' of differing kinds as a punishment for conspiring against Prospero. Alonso in despair wishes to drown himself 'deeper than . . . plummet sounded' and Prospero drowns his book and with it his magic power using the same phrase.

XII

VERSE AND PROSE

The impact of dialogue was enhanced by its traditional verse form; it gave to the major characters an impressive grandeur, a stature larger than life. In Shakespeare's plays its range, power, and flexibility are truly astounding. In addition he uses prose almost as varied in style and force. In Shakespeare's earlier plays couplets are frequently employed for a variety of purposes; in *The Tempest* although some internal rhymes have been noticed, couplets are not used in the normal five-footed line, but they are used in the shorter lines of the masque in IV. i; and rhymes are used in all the songs. The normal speech media are then blank verse and prose.

Shakespeare's blank verse can be elaborate, enriched with swiftly following metaphors, with similes and other figures of speech and devices of style; it can be impressive and ceremonious; it can be plain and direct; it can become exaggerated and violent in boasting, raving, or in frenzied appeals to the heavens. Its rhythms can march with a regular beat, or in the later plays vary infinitely to produce the most subtle effects. Characters use the kind of blank verse appropriate to the dramatic moment and not necessarily the kind consistent with what is known of them elsewhere in the play.

Prospero uses blank verse throughout. Rhythm is lightly stressed, the lines flow into each other, and the heavier pauses occur frequently in the middle of a line. His sentences are involved, at times telescoped and ungrammatical although the sense remains clear. Images are quickly varied, the thought moves rapidly from general statement—sometimes an aphorism or proverb—to a particular instance. The shifting of stress and pauses gives the illusion of natural speech. The outstanding characteristic of Prospero's speeches is the frequent use of parentheses. Their function varies, but sometimes they suggest that Prospero is endowed with a schoolmasterly or an editorial cast of mind! It is interesting that in conversation with Ferdinand in IV. i parentheses are notably absent.

Ferdinand's verse is well-ordered and dignified during his first encounter with Prospero and Miranda and remains so generally. His soliloquy however is unusual. It is based on paradoxical statements with a proverb or two, and the internal movement of the fifteen lines (III. i, 1–15) resembles the movement of a Shakespearean sonnet—an apt prologue to a love scene.

Ariel's blank verse is direct, lively with no long involved sentences except in his denunciation of Alonso (III. iii, 53–82) where the frequent parentheses hint that Prospero may have written his speech for him.

Caliban's use of blank verse even when he is talking with Stephano and Trinculo, although admittedly a few of his replies are in prose, is curious. What function is it intended to have? Some suggest that the verses are the fossil remains of an earlier stratum of writing, of an older play in fact. Is it that he has been well educated by Prospero or does he reverence both Prospero and would-be king Stephano? Perhaps because he is the corrupter of Stephano and Trinculo verse has been given him for this purpose, just as Antonio and Sebastian turn from prose to verse when they conspire against Alonso.

II. i displays most careful and judicious use of verse. When the courtiers hold conversation with the king Alonso they speak in blank verse; but when Antonio and Sebastian are mocking Gonzalo and Adrian and Alonso has gone apart in his grief their exchanges are in prose. Apparently Alonso is attentive when Gonzalo describes his commonwealth. Thus there are three passages of verse separated by two of prose. After Alonso, Gonzalo, and Adrian fall asleep Antonio swiftly develops his conspiracy in sinuous blank verse, fluent and varied by swift transitions and subtle innuendos.

Prose is normally used by comic or low characters as befitting their rank, and by contrast with the verse spoken by courtiers. It is used by women and sometimes by men in familiar conversation, or occasionally for the rational development of some intellectual theme. It can present the stumbling conversation of a Dogberry or Verges, the chop-tongue of Feste, the wit and expressiveness of Benedick and Beatrice, the passion of Shylock, and the pensive mood of Hamlet. Shakespeare's concern was always with dramatic effect. After Cæsar's murder, Shakespeare made Brutus, who elsewhere spoke blank verse, utter a flat, rational uninspired speech to the mob as a sharp contrast to the full power of the blank verse speech he gave Antony.

Here the vigorous, abrupt, breathless prose of the opening scene although imperceptibly gliding into verse in the moment of disaster, a delicate touch, depicts the chaos and confusion on board. The prose in which Antonio and Sebastian conduct their jeering at Gonzalo lowers the tone of the incident and the estimation of the speakers. The only characters who speak prose consistently are Stephano and Trinculo, even finally when they are brought before Alonso their drunkenness leaves them prosaic.

XIII

A NOTE ON DRAMATIC STRUCTURE

The Tempest has no dramatic conflict in the accepted sense, and this has been construed as a weakness in its structure. What happens instead is a kind of transfiguration, an alchemy that transmutes facts into values. Yet the thematic urgency of time in the play is a kind of substitute for the normal conflict. In his other romances Shakespeare had shown the workings of Providence in dramatic action extending over many years with a Chorus to draw attention to the lapse of time. These romances were more narrative in structure than *The Tempest*, their events unfolding in chronological sequence, and they were remote in time, place, and society. However strongly a spectator might be caught up in the dramatic illusion, he was still distanced from the play. In *The Tempest* the time span of events, twelve years, is recapitulated, and then resolved within some three hours. Shakespeare has been praised for thus observing the classical unities of time, place, and action, after failing to do so in *The Winter's Tale*, *Cymbeline*, and *Pericles*. Yet he was well aware of this form since he had used it earlier in the *Comedy of Errors*. He was not aiming at the same things in *The Tempest* as that he intended in those other plays.

The Tempest is strikingly and purposefully contemporary. The events that led to Prospero's exile twelve years before are summed up and so narrated as to belong to and inform the present. The modern character names, the references to recent travellers' tales and voyages ('when we were boys who would have thought . . .') 'Bermoothes', 'in England now' all confirm its contemporary setting. The antiquity and content of the romances has been transformed into the immediacy of *The Tempest*. Shakespeare has taken romance elements and freed them from the chronology of history and the limitations of narrative to create a fantasy instantly and directly relevant to the situation of his audience in the London of James I. By giving Prospero the additional function of Chorus he sought to involve its members even more intimately by drawing them in to identify their views with those of Prospero. Such intense concentration could not have been achieved otherwise.

THE TEMPEST

CHARACTERS

ALONSO, King of Naples
SEBASTIAN, his brother
PROSPERO, the right Duke of Milan
ANTONIO, his brother, the usurping Duke of Milan
FERDINAND, son to the King of Naples
GONZALO, an honest old councillor
ADRIAN and FRANCISCO, lords
CALIBAN, a savage and deformed slave
TRINCULO, a jester
STEPHANO, a drunken butler
MASTER OF A SHIP
BOATSWAIN
MARINERS
MIRANDA, daughter to Prospero
ARIEL, an airy spirit
IRIS
CERES
JUNO $\Big\}$ spirits
NYMPHS
REAPERS

SCENE: *a ship at sea; an uninhabited island*

31

On a ship at sea

S.D. *A . . . heard.* The Elizabethan stage with its two entrance doors and back-stage balcony was not unlike the decks of a galleon seen by the audience looking from the bows towards the cabin doors in the stern-castle.

Thunder was simulated by a cannon ball rolled in a wooden barrel, lightning by gunpowder flashes.

When the play was performed before King James in the Banqueting Hall at Whitehall, there were certainly elaborate sets, possibly a backcloth depicting stormy sea and sky, and there may have been mechanical devices showing moving clouds and waves, as well as making noises of thunder and lightning flashes.

S.D. *Shipmaster . . . Boatswain.* The master had charge of the navigation of the ship. The boatswain was his subordinate officer who directed the seamen to carry out the orders indicated by blasts on the master's whistle. The boatswain and sailors were normally stationed forward, the master and passengers aft.

The Shipmaster may enter on the balcony, or the two may enter from opposite doors urgently.

2   *What cheer?* what's to do? what are your orders?

3   *Good.* The master acknowledges the Boatswain's prompt response. *Speak to,* call up. *yarely,* smartly.

5   *my hearts! cheerly,* my lads, put some life into it.

6   *Take . . . topsail.* Accepted manoeuvre to reduce the drift towards a lee shore, and to gain sea room.

7   *Blow . . . enough,* as long as we have enough sea room, blow wind till you burst.

During these exchanges there is considerable bustle to and fro among the sailors, as yet in an orderly fashion.

S.D. *Enter . . . others.* Do the King and his courtiers enter ceremonially, slowly, distractedly, in agitation, frantically, with dignity and calmness? Alonso perhaps wears a crown to distinguish him, Ferdinand his heir perhaps a smaller circlet of gold.

8-9   *Play the men,* behave like men of courage. Some editors prefer the emendation 'Ply', i.e. keep the men working hard, which fits in with the Boatswain's duty.

11   *Where . . . boatswain?* Perhaps a loud aggressive repetition of Alonso's unanswered question.

ACT ONE

SCENE ONE

A tempestuous noise of thunder and lightning heard
Enter a SHIPMASTER *and a* BOATSWAIN

MASTER: Boatswain!

BOATSWAIN: Here master. What cheer?

MASTER: Good. Speak to the mariners. Fall to't yarely, or we
run ourselves aground. Bestir, bestir.   [*Exit*

Enter MARINERS

BOATSWAIN: Heigh my hearts! cheerly, cheerly my hearts!
yare, yare! Take in the topsail. Tend to the master's whistle.
Blow till thou burst thy wind, if room enough.

Enter ALONSO, SEBASTIAN, ANTONIO, FERDINAND,
GONZALO, *and others*

ALONSO: Good boatswain have care. Where's the master? Play
the men.

BOATSWAIN: I pray now keep below.   10

ANTONIO: Where is the master, boatswain?

The Tempest

12   *Do . . . him?* Sarcastic.

13   *You . . . storm,* i.e. by interrupting the Boatswain's work. Does it also associate the court party with disorder?

15   *roarers,* roaring waves.

16   *Silence.* Is this to check a would-be speaker?

18   *None . . . myself.* Is the Boatswain contemptuous of the King, or is he justified in his reproaches?

19   *councillor,* i.e. a member of the king's council. Folio has 'counsellor'. Gonzalo wears a red or purple robe with a gold chain symbolic of his office as councillor.

19–20 *command . . . work.* The Boatswain 'commands' the crew and 'works' the ship, and he sarcastically uses these words to invite Gonzalo to silence the wind and waves and bring about immediate calm.

20   *work,* (*a*) bring about, (*b*) handle (a ship). *present,* i.e. present storm. Maxwell suggests 'presence' i.e. bring about the peace that is proper in the presence of the king.

22–3 *make . . . hour,* i.e. say your prayers.

25–7 *Methinks . . . gallows.* A reference to the proverb, 'He that is born to be hanged shall never be drowned'.

26   *complexion,* (*a*) appearance, (*b*) disposition.

26–7 *perfect gallows,* ensures that he hangs, fits him perfectly for the gallows.

27–8 *rope . . . destiny,* (*a*) hangman's rope that ends his life, (*b*) the thread of life cut off by the Fates.

28   *cable,* anchor chain. *doth little advantage,* is of little help. Is Gonzalo serious or jesting?

30   *Down . . . topmast.* Lowering or striking the topmast is intended to steady the ship and check the shoreward drift.

31   *Bring . . . main-course,* bring her bows to point into the wind. *A plague.* A long dash to complete a line follows this word in the Folio. Kermode suggests that this signifies that the oaths referred to by Sebastian as blasphemous have been removed by censorship.

33   *office,* the noise we make in working ship.

S.D.   The courtiers presumably get in the Boatswain's way.

36–7 *A . . . dog.* Is Sebastian indignant, justified, snarling, spiteful, arrogant, hot-tempered, foul-mouthed? Is this intended to reveal Sebastian's nature or to condemn the Boatswain of inefficiency and bluster?

39   *insolent.* Is he?

41   *for,* against.

BOATSWAIN: Do you not hear him? You mar our labour. Keep
your cabins. You do assist the storm.

GONZALO: Nay, good, be patient.

BOATSWAIN: When the sea is. Hence! What cares these roarers
for the name of king? To cabin. Silence! Trouble us not.

GONZALO: Good, yet remember whom thou hast aboard.   17

BOATSWAIN: None that I more love than myself. You are a
councillor; if you can command these elements to silence, and
work the peace of the present, we will not hand a rope more.
Use your authority. If you cannot, give thanks you have lived
so long, and make yourself ready in your cabin for the mischance of the hour, if it so hap. Cheerly good hearts! Out of
our way I say.   24
                                                        [*Exit*

GONZALO: I have great comfort from this fellow. Methinks he
hath no drowning mark upon him, his complexion is perfect
gallows. Stand fast, good Fate, to his hanging; make the rope
of his destiny our cable, for our own doth little advantage. If he
be not born to be hanged, our case is miserable.   [*Exeunt*

Enter BOATSWAIN

BOATSWAIN: Down with the topmast. Yare, lower; lower.
Bring her to try with main-course. [*A cry within.*] A plague
upon this howling! They are louder than the weather or our
office.   33

Enter SEBASTIAN, ANTONIO, *and* GONZALO

Yet again? What do you here? Shall we give o'er and drown?
Have you a mind to sink?

SEBASTIAN: A pox o' your throat, you bawling, blasphemous,
incharitable dog!

BOATSWAIN: Work you then.

ANTONIO: Hang, cur, hang, you whoreson, insolent noisemaker.
We are less afraid to be drowned than thou art.   40

GONZALO: I'll warrant him for drowning, though the ship were

35

44   *Lay her a-hold*. 'a-hold' is probably intended for 'a-hull', i.e. heave the boat to with her bows into the wind. *set . . . courses*, set two sails, the foresail as well as the mainsail. The Boatswain makes a last desperate attempt to work the ship away from the island.

S.D.   *Enter Mariners wet*. How do they enter—turbulently, frantically, in clusters, trailing exhaustedly, frenziedly?

46   *All . . . lost*. Is this shouted in unison or individually?

      What movements are appropriate—clasping hands, kneeling, throwing themselves down, raising hands appealingly, clinging together?

47   *cold*, i.e. in death. Some referring to 'drunkards' (l. 50), and 'wide-chapped' (l. 51) suggest that the Boatswain takes a swig from a bottle of sack.

49   *out of patience*. Sebastian and Antonio lack the virtue prescribed to christians in tribulation, neither are they prayerful.

50   *merely*, utterly.

51   *wide-chapped*, wide mouthed.

51–2   *lie . . . tides*. Pirates were hanged on the shore at low tide and their bodies left until three high tides had covered them.

53   *swear*. Perhaps the roaring and threatening of the waves.

54   *glut*, swallow.

54–5   *Mercy . . . split*. How can this be made convincing—by bringing some in frenzy on deck, by confusing the cries, by adding other noises and screams to the cries?

58   *Let's . . . him*. Is this spoken disgustedly, furiously, with dignity, courageously?

60   *long heath*. A particular kind of heath plant. *brown furze*, i.e. dead furze. Some prefer to read 'broom, furze'.

61   *dry death*. Perhaps a spirited jest, i.e. without all this watery accompaniment. A 'dry death' according to Jeremy Taylor was one unaccompanied by weeping.

      What may be inferred from this scene—beyond its noise and spectacle—that the anger of the heavens is being visited on guilty men, that the courtiers are being shocked into revealing their true natures by the approach of death, that the storm establishes Prospero's supernatural power as it were in advance, that the chaos in the sky and sea reflects a breaking down of social order among the human beings on the ship, that the storm is a device to cover up the noise of latecomers into the theatre, that it is a rousing no stronger than a nutshell, and as leaky as an unstanched wench.

BOATSWAIN: Lay her a-hold, a-hold; set her two courses off to sea again; lay her off.

Enter MARINERS *wet*

MARINERS: All lost, to prayers, to prayers! All lost!

BOATSWAIN: What, must our mouths be cold?

GONZALO: The King and Prince at prayers, let's assist them, for our case is as theirs.

SEBASTIAN: I'm out of patience.

ANTONIO: We are merely cheated of our lives by drunkards.   50
This wide-chapped rascal—would thou mightst lie drowning
The washing of ten tides.

GONZALO: He'll be hanged yet,
Though every drop of water swear against it,
And gape at wid'st to glut him.
        [*A confused noise within*. Mercy on us!—
We split, we split—Farewell my wife and children—
Farewell brother—We split, we split, we split.]

ANTONIO: Let's all sink wi' th' King.   57

SEBASTIAN: Let's take leave of him.

                                        [*Exeunt Antonio and Sebastian*

GONZALO: Now would I give a thousand furlongs of sea for an acre of barren ground, long heath, brown furze, any thing. The wills above be done, but I would fain die a dry death.

                                                            [*Exeunt*

spectacle that leaves the audience startled and in suspense about the
fate of all on the ship, that the title of the play indicates that this
scene is significant?

The Island. Before Prospero's cell

On the public stage Prospero's cell would be the 'discovery space'
under the balcony, or a 'mansion' constructed in front of the rear
wall.

For the royal performance it could be arranged with stage rocks
on the raised back stage. Are any other properties required?

How do they enter—Prospero first alone in meditation to
whom Miranda runs, Prospero leading Miranda by hand,
Miranda clutching his robe, etc.?

Prospero's robe should indicate that he is a magician by
alchemical, zodiacal, or cabbalistic signs. He may have a wand.

How should Miranda be clothed—in garments tattered by
twelve years' wear, in splendid contemporary costume, in a
richly coloured robe, in a white simple garment?

1   *art*, magical power.

1–2   *If . . . them.* Is it an anti-climax to know that the storm is 'artificial',
      does it deepen the mystery and suspense, does it indicate Prospero
      as a good magician who can restore order and harmony as well as
      cause them?

4–5   *But . . . out.* This image of conflict between sea and sky and their
      chaotic rebellious mingling occurs frequently in Shakespeare.

4   *welkin's cheek*, expanse of heavens. See *Coriolanus*, V. iii, 151.
      Dover Wilson suggests that 'cheek' = 'the side of a grate'.

5–7   *O . . . her.* Is Miranda distraught, hysterical, tearful, naive,
      optimistic, tender, indignant, pitiful? Any gestures to mark her
      feelings?

6   *brave*, fine, splendid.

7   *noble creature.* In what sense is Miranda using 'noble'?

10   *Had . . . power.* Another indirect acknowledgment of Prospero's
      power.

13   *fraughting*, with which she was laden. Does Prospero reduce the
      storm? *collected*, calm.

14   *amazement*, alarm, bewilderment. *piteous*, full of pity.

15   *O . . . day.* Miranda is not easily consoled. To the audience
      Prospero's assurance that no harm has been done is mystifying and
      sharpens expectations.

SCENE TWO

Enter PROSPERO *and* MIRANDA

MIRANDA: If by your art, my dearest father, you have
    Put the wild waters in this roar, allay them.
    The sky, it seems, would pour down stinking pitch,
    But that the sea, mounting to the welkin's cheek,
    Dashes the fire out. O I have suffered
    With those that I saw suffer. A brave vessel,
    Who had no doubt some noble creature in her,
    Dashed all to pieces. O the cry did knock
    Against my very heart. Poor souls, they perished.
    Had I been any god of power, I would   10
    Have sunk the sea within the earth, or ere
    It should the good ship so have swallowed, and
    The fraughting souls within her.
PROSPERO: Be collected;
    No more amazement. Tell your piteous heart
    There's no harm done.
MIRANDA: O woe the day!
PROSPERO: No harm.

16–17 *I . . . daughter.* Further explanation that again excites curiosity.

17 *thee . . . daughter.* What does the repetition of 'thee' imply— affection, tenderness, firm insistence, teasing?

20 *full,* very.

22 *meddle,* mingle, i.e. did not occur to me, or did not trouble my mind.

22–3 *'Tis . . . further.* Prospero acts rather as the Presenter in a masque who explains how the situation has arisen.

23–5 *Lend . . . art.* Why does Prospero remove his magic robe—because his story has no need of magic, to symbolize the 'artlessness' of his story, to reassure both Miranda and the audience that he is human, to rouse the audience's sympathy and understanding?
   Does Prospero sit or remain standing? See l. 32.

26 *direful,* dreadful.

27 *virtue,* essence, spirit.

28 *provision,* foresight. Editors accept this emendation for the Folio reading 'compassion', which it is presumed was set up by the compositor who misread it from the previous line. It might be thought however that 'compassion' could carry a quibble on 'compass' to contrive, to bring about.

29 *soul,* i.e. soul lost. Dover Wilson suggests 'soil'. (See II. i, 59–61.)

31 *Betid,* happened.

33–6 *You . . . yet.* Does this suggest a restraint?

35 *bootless inquisition,* empty curiosity, unsatisfied wish to know more. Does this contradict ll. 21–2?

37 *The . . . ear.* The urgency of the moment is repeatedly stressed (ll. 23, 181–4). The climax of an enchantment normally demanded a favourable moment. It serves also to increase the tension of the story.

41 *out,* fully.

I have done nothing but in care of thee,
Of thee my dear one, thee my daughter, who
Art ignorant of what thou art, nought knowing
Of whence I am, nor that I am more better
Than Prospero, master of a full poor cell,   20
And thy no greater father.

MIRANDA: More to know
Did never meddle with my thoughts.

PROSPERO: 'Tis time
I should inform thee further. Lend thy hand,
And pluck my magic garment from me. So.

                                    [*Lays down his mantle*

Lie there, my art. Wipe thou thine eyes, have comfort.
The direful spectacle of the wreck, which touched
The very virtue of compassion in thee,
I have with such provision in mine art
So safely ordered, that there is no soul—
No, not so much perdition as an hair   30
Betid to any creature in the vessel
Which thou heard'st cry, which thou saw'st sink. Sit down,
For thou must now know further.

MIRANDA: You have often
Begun to tell me what I am, but stopped,
And left me to a bootless inquisition,
Concluding, 'Stay, not yet'.

PROSPERO: The hour's now come,
The very minute bids thee ope thine ear.
Obey, and be attentive. Canst thou remember
A time before we came unto this cell?
I do not think thou canst, for then thou wast not   40
Out three years old.

MIRANDA: Certainly sir, I can.

PROSPERO: By what? By any other house or person?
Of any thing the image, tell me, that

45   *assurance*, certainty.
46   *warrants*, testifies, guarantees.

50   *backward*, past. *abysm*, abyss.

53–5   *Twelve . . . power.* Spoken impressively and emphatically.
53   *since*, ago.

56   *piece*, masterpiece, the perfection.
57–8   *thy . . . Milan.* Is this elaboration and repetition an attempt to meet Miranda's incredulity, facetiousness, a tender or smarting reminiscence or to establish very clearly Miranda's noble birth?
59   *And.* Some emend to 'A'. *no worse issued*, no humbler in birth.

62–3   *By . . . hither.* The antithesis is sharpened by alliteration 'heaved', 'holp'.
63   *blessedly*, i.e. by Providence. See l. 159. *holp*, helped.
63–4   *O . . . to.* Does Prospero show any signs of emotion? Does Miranda make any gesture of sympathy or affection?
64   *teen*, grief, trouble.

67–8   *I . . . perfidious.* Strife between brothers was held to be one of the worst crimes. Compare *Hamlet, As You Like It, Richard III.*

70   *my state*, the affairs of my dukedom. *as at*, at.
71   *signories*, states, dukedoms. *the first*, supreme.

Hath kept with thy remembrance.

MIRANDA: 'Tis far off,
And rather like a dream than an assurance
That my remembrance warrants. Had I not
Four or five women once that tended me?

PROSPERO: Thou hadst, and more Miranda. But how is it
That this lives in thy mind? What seest thou else
In the dark backward and abysm of time?   50
If thou remembrest aught ere thou cam'st here,
How thou cam'st here thou mayst.

MIRANDA: But that I do not.

PROSPERO: Twelve year since, Miranda, twelve year since,
Thy father was the Duke of Milan and
A prince of power.

MIRANDA: Sir, are not you my father?

PROSPERO: Thy mother was a piece of virtue, and
She said thou wast my daughter; and thy father
Was Duke of Milan; and his only heir,
And princess, no worse issued.

MIRANDA: O the heavens,
What foul play had we, that we came from thence?   60
Or blessed was't we did?

PROSPERO: Both, both my girl.
By foul play, as thou say'st, were we heaved thence,
But blessedly holp hither.

MIRANDA: O my heart bleeds
To think o' th' teen that I have turned you to,
Which is from my remembrance. Please you further.

PROSPERO: My brother and thy uncle, called Antonio—
I pray thee mark me, that a brother should
Be so perfidious—he whom next thyself
Of all the world I loved, and to him put
The manage of my state; as at that time   70
Through all the signories it was the first,

72   *prime*, foremost.

73   *In dignity*, in rank. *liberal arts*, free humane studies, branches of knowledge.

74   *study*, interest, occupation.

76   *state*, public position, affairs of state.

76-7 *transported and rapt*, absorbed and involved.

77   *secret studies*, studies of the hidden powers of nature. *secret*, (*a*) private, (*b*) abstruse. Possibly this hints at studies of magic.

78   *Dost . . . heedfully*. Miranda's inattention in this scene has roused much speculation about its origin. Is she—sleepy, uninterested, distracted by something else, bemused? Is she untruthful when she asserts that she is attending? Is Prospero emotionally roused in his story and trying to rouse Miranda too—successfully after l. 115? Is it a dramatic device to break up a long narrative that might send King James and the audience to sleep? Is it an indication that Prospero is no longer the absorbed student, but an active director of affairs.

79-81 *Being . . . over-topping*, having learnt the art of granting or refusing requests, of choosing some for promotion and holding in check others who presumptuously exceeded their powers.

81   *trash*, check (a dog by a leash).

83   *key*, (*a*) key to a lock, (*b*) key in music.

84-5 *set . . . ear*. 'set', 'tune', 'ear' continue the music image from 'key'.

85   *now*, by this time.

86-7 *The . . . on't*. Ivy was regarded as 'usurping' (*Comedy of Errors*, II. ii, 180), and was associated with ambition. It was an adornment of the emblem figure of Ambition (Ripa, *Iconologia*).

87   *verdure*, vigour, authority. Is Prospero restless, indignantly gesticulating, or speaking almost to himself?

87-8 *Thou . . . do*. See above l. 78.

89   *wordly ends*, i.e. the practical affairs of my dukedom.

90-2 *closeness . . . rate*, seclusion to study more deeply those things which, except that they were so abstract, were far beyond the value popularly allowed them. Some consider that Prospero had virtually abdicated his rectorship.

93-6 *and . . . was*. Two proverbs combined to give force to the point: 'Trust begets treason', 'A father above common rate has usually a son below it'.

97-9 *He . . . exact*. He being invested with authority maintained not

44

And Prospero the prime duke, being so reputed
In dignity, and for the liberal arts
Without a parallel; those being all my study,
The government I cast upon my brother,
And to my state grew stranger, being transported
And rapt in secret studies. Thy false uncle—
Dost thou attend me?

MIRANDA: Sir, most heedfully.

PROSPERO: Being once perfected how to grant suits,
  How to deny them, who t' advance, and who   80
  To trash for over-topping, new created
  The creatures that were mine, I say, or changed 'em,
  Or else new formed 'em; having both the key
  Of officer and office, set all hearts i' th' state
  To what tune pleased his ear; that now he was
  The ivy which had hid my princely trunk,
  And sucked my verdure out on 't. Thou attend'st not.

MIRANDA: O good sir, I do.

PROSPERO: I pray thee mark me.
  I thus neglecting wordly ends, all dedicated
  To closeness and the bettering of my mind   90
  With that which, but by being so retired,
  O'er-prized all popular rate, in my false brother
  Awaked an evil nature; and my trust,
  Like a good parent, did beget of him
  A falsehood in its contrary as great
  As my trust was, which had indeed no limit,
  A confidence sans bound. He being thus lorded,
  Not only with what my revenue yielded,
  But what my power might else exact, like one

only by the incomes of my estate but also by the exploitation of my power.

100   *into.* Some editors prefer 'unto'.

      The general sense of these lines is: like a man who by constantly repeating a lie, so corrupted his memory by supporting the lie, that finally he came to believe that his lie was the truth, i.e. that he was in fact the duke.

103–5 *out . . . prerogative*, arising from his office as my deputy and his performing, with all its privileges and dignities, the public duties of royalty.

107–8 *To . . . for*, (ambitious) to have no distinction between playing the part of the duke and being the duke in reality.

109   *Absolute Milan*, the absolute ruler of Milan.

109–   *Me . . . enough.* Is this Antonio's contemptuous opinion or
10   Prospero's reminiscence?

110   *temporal royalties*, worldy royal duties.

112   *dry*, thirsty. Ambition was associated with the 'choler a-dust' i.e. a hot dry humour. Choler was associated also with bitterness and destructiveness.

117   *condition*, agreement made with the king of Naples. *event*, outcome.

117–   *then . . . brother.* Is Prospero—indignant, sarcastic, ironic, mourn-
18   ful, intense?

118   *a brother*, a brotherly act.

119   *but*, other than.

123–4 *in . . . tribute*, in return for specified acts of homage and a large sum of tribute money.

125   *presently*, straightway.

Who having into truth, by telling of it,   100
Made such a sinner of his memory,
To credit his own lie, he did believe
He was indeed the duke; out o' th' substitution,
And executing the outward face of royalty,
With all prerogative; hence his ambition growing—
Dost thou hear?

MIRANDA: Your tale, sir, would cure deafness.

PROSPERO: To have no screen between this part he played
And him he played it for, he needs will be
Absolute Milan. Me, poor man, my library
Was dukedom large enough: of temporal royalties   110
He thinks me now incapable; confederates—
So dry he was for sway—wi' th' King of Naples
To give him annual tribute, do him homage,
Subject his coronet to his crown, and bend
The dukedom yet unbowed—alas, poor Milan!—
To most ignoble stooping.

MIRANDA: O the heavens!

PROSPERO: Mark his condition, and the event, then tell me
If this might be a brother.

MIRANDA: I should sin
To think but nobly of my grandmother:
Good wombs have borne bad sons.

PROSPERO: Now the condition.   120
This King of Naples being an enemy
To me inveterate, hearkens my brother's suit,
Which was, that he in lieu o' th' premises
Of homage, and I know not how much tribute,
Should presently extirpate me and mine
Out of the dukedom, and confer fair Milan
With all the honours on my brother. Whereon,
A treacherous army levied, one midnight
Fated to the purpose, did Antonio open

47

130   *dead*, silent time.
131   *ministers*, those especially selected. 'Minister' in Shakespeare often
       seems to have either a heavenly or hellish association. Here it
       implies evil agents.

134   *hint*, occasion.
135   *wrings mine eyes*, wrinkles up my eyelids, squeezes tears from my
       eyes. Is Miranda unduly tearful? See I. ii, 25; III. i, 11–12.

138   *impertinent*, pointless.

142   *A . . . bloody*, i.e. as hunters were 'blooded' after a deer was
       killed. See *Julius Cæsar*, III. i, 205–6.
143   *colours*, (*a*) false appearances, (*b*) hues. *fairer*, (*a*) more apparently
       just, (*b*) more pleasing than blood red.
144   *few*, few words.
146   *carcass*, skeleton frame of a ship. *butt*. 'Contemptuously for a
       "tub of a boat"' (Kermode). Falconar thinks that there is some-
       thing to be said for 'buss', a fishing vessel.
148   *hoist*, embarked.
150–1 *whose . . . wrong*. For the association of 'winds', 'pity' and 'cheru-
       bin' (l. 152) see *Macbeth*, I. vii, 21–5. The image may have been
       suggested by contemporary maps with their cherubic heads
       blowing the winds.
151   *loving wrong*, i.e. the winds though blowing sighs of pity en-
       dangered us.
152   *cherubin*, i.e. young, innocent, and beautiful. The word carries
       many associations apt to the situation: (*a*) with God's presence
       (l. 159), (*b*) in Shakespeare with patience and endurance (*Othello*,
       IV. ii, 64), (*c*) and in the *Old Testament* with wind (*Psalms* xviii.
       10) where they bear the Lord upon 'the wings of the wind'.
       (See also Helen Gardner, *Business of Criticism*, pp. 53–60.)

The gates of Milan, and i' th' dead of darkness,   130
The ministers for th' purpose hurried thence
Me and thy crying self.

MIRANDA: Alack, for pity!
I not rememb'ring how I cried out then,
Will cry it o'er again. It is a hint
That wrings mine eyes to 't.

PROSPERO: Hear a little further,
And then I'll bring thee to the present business
Which now's upon's; without the which this story
Were most impertinent.

MIRANDA: Wherefore did they not
That hour destroy us?

PROSPERO: Well demanded, wench;
My tale provokes that question. Dear, they durst not,   140
So dear the love my people bore me; nor set
A mark so bloody on the business; but
With colours fairer painted their foul ends.
In few, they hurried us aboard a bark,
Bore us some leagues to sea, where they prepared
A rotten carcass of a butt, not rigged,
Nor tackle, sail, nor mast; the very rats
Instinctively have quit it. There they hoist us,
To cry to the sea that roared to us, to sigh
To the winds whose pity, sighing back again,   150
Did us but loving wrong.

MIRANDA: Alack, what trouble
Was I then to you.

PROSPERO: O, a cherubin
Thou wast that did preserve me. Thou didst smile,
Infused with a fortitude from heaven,

155 *decked*, (*a*) covered, (*b*) adorned. Some refer to a dialect word 'deg', to sprinkle.

156 *which*, i.e. Miranda's smile.

157 *undergoing stomach*, enduring courage.

159 *By Providence divine*. An impressive short line. See l. 63.

162 *charity*, christian charity.

163 *design*, plot.

164 *stuffs*, materials.

165 *steaded much*, stood us in good stead. *gentleness*, noble qualities.

167–8 *volumes . . . dukedom*, i.e. books dealing with magic. See III. ii, 86–9; V. i, 57.

169 *Now I arise*. Some assume that Prospero stands and puts on his magic robe; others that he knows that he is rising from misfortune to the top of Fortune's wheel. See ll. 178–9.

170 *Sit still*, i.e. continue to sit.

172–4 *made . . . careful*, given you the advantages of an education better than that obtainable by princesses who spend more time in trivialities, and whose teachers are less conscientious.

176 *beating . . . mind*. See IV. i, 163; V. i, 246.

178 *accident*, chance, happening according to fortune. *strange*, wonderful. *Fortune*. The goddess, Fortune, was depicted as blindfold, standing on a rolling ball, and turning a wheel upon which men's fortunes depended. She was regarded as God's agent.

181 *zenith*, the highest point of good fortune from the astrological aspect.

182 *auspicious*, favourable. *influence*, i.e. of the stars over his destiny.

When I have decked the sea with drops full salt,
Under my burden groaned; which raised in me
An undergoing stomach, to bear up
Against what should ensue.

MIRANDA: How came we ashore?

PROSPERO: By Providence divine.
Some food we had, and some fresh water that   160
A noble Neapolitan, Gonzalo,
Out of his charity, who being then appointed
Master of this design, did give us, with
Rich garments, linens, stuffs, and necessaries,
Which since have steaded much; so of his gentleness,
Knowing I loved my books, he furnished me
From mine own library with volumes that
I prize above my dukedom.

MIRANDA: Would I might
But ever see that man.

PROSPERO: Now I arise.   [*Resumes his mantle*
Sit still, and hear the last of our sea-sorrow.   170
Here in this island we arrived, and here
Have I, thy schoolmaster, made thee more profit
Than other princesses can, that have more time
For vainer hours, and tutors not so careful.

MIRANDA: Heavens thank you for 't. And now I pray you sir,
For still 'tis beating in my mind, your reason
For raising this sea-storm?

PROSPERO: Know thus far forth.
By accident most strange, bountiful Fortune,
Now my dear lady, hath mine enemies
Brought to this shore. And by my prescience   180
I find my zenith doth depend upon
A most auspicious star, whose influence

183   *omit*, neglect to take advantage of, disregard. Prospero's opportunity is limited to the short period when the star is auspicious.

184–6   *Here . . . choose.* Presumably Prospero charms Miranda to sleep. Any movements or gestures?

185   *good dulness*, i.e. a healthy sleepiness.

187   *Come . . . come.* Any movements or gestures to summon Ariel?

S.D.   *Enter Ariel.* Is Ariel a boy, man or woman? He was probably clad symbolically in a silken tunic of rainbow colours, wings to match, blue silk stockings and buskins and a coronet of flowers. How should he enter—normally, swiftly, through a trap-door, or by machine from above?

189–   *All . . . bidding.* Ariel's ceremonious greeting establishes Prospero's
92   authority, dignity, and mastery of magical arts.

189   *great master*, i.e. of magic.

192   *task*, employ.

193   *quality*, (*a*) fellow spirits, (*b*) powers. Ariel's description of his powers prepares the audience for his answer to Prospero's question.

194   *to point*, in every detail.

196   *beak*, the long pointed prow of Elizabethan ships.

198   *flamed amazement*, my appearance as flames struck all with fear and wonder.

200   *distinctly*, in several places at the same time. Ariel describes St Elmo's fire, a discharge of static electricity, referred to in the travel books of the period.

204   *sulphurous*, fiery and thunderous. *Neptune.* In Roman myth the god of the seas. Ariel speaks with obvious pleasure. Any illustrative action or gestures?

206   *brave*, fine, excellent.

207   *coil*, tumult, uproar.

208   *infect his reason*, affect, break down, his sanity.

209   *fever . . . mad*, frenzy such as madmen feel. The storm that Prospero raised in sky and sea has a complementary disturbance in the minds of those on the ship. See Introduction, pp. 11-14.

If now I court not, but omit, my fortunes
Will ever after droop. Here cease more questions;
Thou art inclined to sleep. 'T is a good dulness,
And give it way. I know thou canst not choose.

[Miranda sleeps

Come away, servant, come. I am ready now.
Approach my Ariel, come.

Enter ARIEL

ARIEL: All hail, great master! Grave sir, hail! I come
   To answer thy best pleasure; be 't to fly,   190
   To swim, to dive into the fire, to ride
   On the curled clouds; to thy strong bidding task
   Ariel, and all his quality.
PROSPERO: Hast thou, spirit,
   Performed to point the tempest that I bade thee?
ARIEL: To every article.
   I boarded the King's ship; now on the beak,
   Now in the waist, the deck, in every cabin,
   I flamed amazement. Sometime I'd divide,
   And burn in many places; on the topmast,
   The yards and bowsprit, would I flame distinctly,   200
   Then meet and join. Jove's lightnings, the precursors
   O' th' dreadful thunder-claps, more momentary
   And sight-outrunning were not; the fire and cracks
   Of sulphurous roaring the most mighty Neptune
   Seem to besiege, and make his bold waves tremble,
   Yea, his dread trident shake.
PROSPERO: My brave spirit,
   Who was so firm, so constant, that this coil
   Would not infect his reason?
ARIEL: Not a soul
   But felt a fever of the mad, and played

211–   *vessel . . . me*. Some editors prefer the Folio punctuation which is a
12   semicolon after 'vessel', and no mark after 'me'.

213   *With . . . reeds*, standing on end like reeds growing in a reed bed.

217   *Not . . . perished*. See l. 30. Editors refer to St Paul's shipwreck for
       the phrase, *Acts*, xxvii. 34. The phrase, however, is common in
       the Bible.

218–   *On . . . before*. See II. i, 59–61.
19

223   *odd angle*, solitary corner.

224   *in . . . knot*, folded in this sorrowful way. Folded arms were a
       sign of grief. Ariel illustrates—mockingly or sympathetically?

224–6 *Of . . . fleet*. Kermode notes that Prospero is an impatient speaker.

227   *nook*, inlet.

228   *fetch dew*. Dew used for magic charms had to be gathered at mid-
       night. See l. 321.

229   *still-vexed*, ever stormy. *Bermoothes*, Bermudas, then notorious
       for storms and witchcraft.

231   *suffered labour*, toil they have endured.

234   *flote*, sea.

Some tricks of desperation. All but mariners 210
Plunged in the foaming brine, and quit the vessel,
Then all afire with me. The King's son Ferdinand,
With hair up-staring—then like reeds, not hair—
Was the first man that leaped; cried, 'Hell is empty,
And all the devils are here'.

PROSPERO: Why, that 's my spirit.
But was not this nigh shore?

ARIEL: Close by, my master.

PROSPERO: But are they, Ariel, safe?

ARIEL: Not a hair perished;
On their sustaining garments not a blemish,
But fresher than before. And, as thou bad'st me,
In troops I have dispersed them 'bout the isle. 220
The King's son have I landed by himself,
Whom I left cooling of the air with sighs
In an odd angle of the isle, and sitting,
His arms in this sad knot.

PROSPERO: Of the King's ship,
The mariners, say how thou hast disposed,
And all the rest o' th' fleet.

ARIEL: Safely in harbour
Is the King's ship; in the deep nook, where once
Thou call'dst me up at midnight to fetch dew
From the still-vexed Bermoothes, there she's hid;
The mariners all under hatches stowed, 230
Who, with a charm joined to their suffered labour,
I have left asleep. And for the rest o' th' fleet,
Which I dispersed, they all have met again,
And are upon the Mediterranean flote,
Bound sadly home for Naples,
Supposing that they saw the King's ship wrecked,
And his great person perish.

PROSPERO: Ariel, thy charge

240   *two glasses*. Ariel is vague, perhaps resentfully, and Prospero defines the time more precisely. For the frequent references to time in the play see Introduction, pp. 9–10.

241   *most preciously*, i.e. with care as it is most valuable.

242   *pains*, tasks.

243   *remember*, remind.

244   *me*, for me. *Moody*, discontented, rebellious.

250   *bate me*, reduce my service by.

251–2 *No. Thou dost*. Is Prospero right or is this a mere device to recount Ariel's history?

255   *veins o' th' earth*, water courses in the earth like veins in the body. A contemporary belief.

256   *baked*, hardened. The word was used quite normally of frost-bound objects.

257   *malignant*, resentful, discontented, rebellious.

258   *Sycorax*. Possibly the name is associated with *corax*, a raven; Caliban, moreover, mentions a raven's feather used by his mother for her charms. In addition it might relate to the enchantress Circe, a Colchian of the tribe of Coraxi, who was exiled on to an island in the Mediterranean.

261   *Argier*, Algiers. *O . . . so*. Prospero is sarcastic, but does not say where she was born. Dover Wilson suggests that the text has been cut.

Exactly is performed. But there's more work.
What is the time o' th' day?

ARIEL: Past the mid season.

PROSPERO: At least two glasses. The time 'twixt six and now
Must by us both be spent most preciously.   241

ARIEL: Is there more toil? Since thou dost give me pains,
Let me remember thee what thou hast promised,
Which is not yet performed me.

PROSPERO: How now? Moody?
What is 't thou canst demand?

ARIEL: My liberty.

PROSPERO: Before the time be out? No more.

ARIEL: I prithee,
Remember I have done thee worthy service,
Told thee no lies, made thee no mistakings, served
Without or grudge or grumblings; thou didst promise
To bate me a full year.

PROSPERO: Dost thou forget   250
From what a torment I did free thee?

ARIEL: No.

PROSPERO: Thou dost, and think'st it much to tread the ooze
Of the salt deep,
To run upon the sharp wind of the north,
To do me business in the veins o' th' earth
When it is baked with frost.

ARIEL: I do not sir.

PROSPERO: Thou liest, malignant thing. Hast thou forgot
The foul witch Sycorax, who with age and envy
Was grown into a hoop? Hast thou forgot her?

ARIEL: No sir.

PROSPERO: Thou hast. Where was she born? Speak; tell
     me.   260

ARIEL: Sir, in Argier.

PROSPERO: O, was she so? I must

263 *damned*, i.e. to hell.

266–7 *for . . . life*. Again Prospero does not say what it was.

269 *blue-eyed*, (*a*) deep sunken, blue-ringed eyes, (*b*) blue-lidded eyes were believed to indicate pregnancy.

271 *As . . . thyself*. Sarcasm or noting an admission?

272–3 *spirit . . . commands*. Ariel is an 'airy spirit', mainly composed of and active in, the 'element' of air.

274 *grand hests*, powerful commands.

275 *potent ministers*, evil spirits summoned by witchcraft.

281 *strike*, i.e. the noise of the buckets hitting the water.

282 *litter*, give birth to, like an animal.

283 *freckled*. Possibly an indication of evil. Error in the *Faerie Queene* has a speckled tail. *whelp*, offspring of a noxious being.

284 *Yes . . . son*. Is this said with eager agreement, sulky insolence, disagreement with Prospero?

285 *Dull . . . so*. Is Prospero stressing the information, or annoyed at Ariel's interruption?

291 *mine art*, i.e. my good (white) magic.

Once in a month recount what thou has been,
Which thou forget'st. This damned witch Sycorax,
For mischiefs manifold, and sorceries terrible
To enter human hearing, from Argier,
Thou know'st was banished: for one thing she did
They would not take her life. Is not this true?

ARIEL: Ay sir.

PROSPERO: This blue-eyed hag was hither brought with child,
    And here was left by the sailors. Thou my slave,   270
    As thou report'st thyself, wast then her servant;
    And for thou wast a spirit too delicate
    To act her earthy and abhorred commands,
    Refusing her grand hests, she did confine thee
    By help of her more potent ministers,
    And in her most unmitigable rage,
    Into a cloven pine; within which rift
    Imprisoned thou didst painfully remain
    A dozen years; within which space she died,
    And left thee there; where thou didst vent thy groans   280
    As fast as mill-wheels strike. Then was this island—
    Save for the son that she did litter here,
    A freckled whelp hag-born—not honoured with
    A human shape.

ARIEL: Yes, Caliban her son.

PROSPERO: Dull thing, I say so; he, that Caliban
    Whom now I keep in service. Thou best know'st
    What torment I did find thee in; thy groans
    Did make wolves howl, and penetrate the breasts
    Of ever-angry bears. It was a torment
    To lay upon the damned, which Sycorax   290
    Could not again undo. It was mine art,
    When I arrived and heard thee, that made gape
    The pine, and let thee out.

ARIEL: I thank thee master.

296–8 *Pardon . . . gently.* Any gesture or movement?

297 *correspondent*, obedient.

298 *spriting*, work as a spirit. *gently*, politely, without complaint.

299 *That's . . . master*, that is spoken like my generous master.

301–3 *make . . . else.* What is the point of this if Ariel is not to be seen by any other stage-character? In the masque *Tethys' Festival* a sea-nymph wore sea-green silk with a silver embroidery of waves with a dressing of reeds. (Nicoll.)

303 *shape*, (*a*) appearance, (*b*) stage costume (Mahood).

304 *diligence*, speed.

306–7 *The . . . me.* Is this likely? Perhaps Miranda can think of no other natural explanation. Should we interpret, 'Your story had the curious effect of making me drowsy'?

311 *miss*, do without.

312– *offices . . . us*, duties to our advantage. For Caliban as an image of
13   the vegetable soul see Introduction. pp. 9, 21.

313– *What . . . speak.* Where is Caliban—under stage, within a cave in
14   the wings or back-stage?

314 *Thou earth.* An indication of Caliban's nature by contrast with Ariel's airyness. *There's . . . within.* Is Caliban's voice—slurred, hoarse, gruff, slobbery, snarling? His speaking unseen whets anticipation of his appearance.

316 *tortoise.* A symbol of ignorance as well as of sloth.

PROSPERO : If thou more murmur'st, I will rend an oak,
    And peg thee in his knotty entrails, till
    Thou hast howled away twelve winters.
ARIEL :   Pardon, master,
    I will be correspondent to command,
    And do my spriting gently.
PROSPERO :   Do so, and after two days
    I will discharge thee.
ARIEL :   That's my noble master.
    What shall I do? Say what. What shall I do?   300
PROSPERO : Go make thyself like a nymph o' the sea. Be subject
    To no sight but thine and mine, invisible
    To every eyeball else. Go take this shape
    And hither come in 't. Go. Hence with diligence.

                                                    [*Exit Ariel*

    Awake, dear heart awake, thou hast slept well;
    Awake.
MIRANDA : The strangeness of your story put
    Heaviness in me.
PROSPERO :   Shake it off. Come on,
    We 'll visit Caliban my slave, who never
    Yields us kind answer.
MIRANDA :   'T is a villain, sir,
    I do not love to look on.
PROSPERO :   But as 't is,   310
    We cannot miss him. He does make our fire,
    Fetch in our wood, and serves in offices
    That profit us. What ho! Slave! Caliban!
    Thou earth, thou! Speak.
CALIBAN :   [*Within*] There's wood enough within.
PROSPERO : Come forth, I say, there's other business for thee.
    Come thou tortoise, when?

317   *quaint*, ingenious, dainty.

       Ariel's return adds further suspense to the audience waiting for the spectacle of Caliban.

319– *got . . . dam*, i.e. Caliban's father was the Devil, his mother,
20   Sycorax, a witch.

S.D.   *Enter Caliban.* What is Caliban's shape, colouring—fish-like, ape-like, freckled, dark, hairy, smooth, tailless, deformed? Does he walk, crawl, shamble, shuffle, crouch? Is he a 'woodwose'? (See Introduction, p. 21.) Does Miranda show any sign of loathing, repugnance, fear, or contempt?

321   *wicked . . . mother.* Perhaps a retort to Prospero's 'wicked dam'. Witches gathered dew by night for their spells.

322   *raven's feather.* The raven, a bird of ill-omen, was associated with witchcraft, and its wings were thought to spread disease. See note to l. 258.

323   *south-west.* Believed to bring diseases.

326   *pen . . . up*, make you gasp for breath. *urchins*, (*a*) goblins, malicious night spirits, (*b*) hedgehogs. Hence, as Kermode notes, 'goblins in the shape of hedgehogs'.

328   *exercise*, work their will.

330   *'em*, honeycomb cells.

331   *This . . . mother.* Is Caliban right?

334   *Water . . . in't.* Unidentified—perhaps wine.

335–6 *bigger . . . night.* An echo of *Genesis*, i. 16. Perhaps a hint at a primitive, Eden-like, state.

337   *qualities*, properties, good things.

339   *charms.* Evil spells worked through the creatures named.

Act One, Scene Two

Enter ARIEL *like a water-nymph*

Fine apparition. My quaint Ariel,
Hark in thine ear.

ARIEL: My lord, it shall be done.   [*Exit*

PROSPERO: Thou poisonous slave, got by the devil himself
    Upon thy wicked dam, come forth.   320

Enter CALIBAN

CALIBAN: As wicked dew as e'er my mother brushed
    With raven's feather from unwholesome fen
    Drop on you both. A south-west blow on ye,
    And blister you all o'er.

PROSPERO: For this, be sure, tonight thou shalt have cramps,
    Side-stitches that shall pen thy breath up; urchins
    Shall, for that vast of night that they may work,
    All exercise on thee; thou shalt be pinched
    As thick as honeycomb, each pinch more stinging
    Than bees that made 'em.

CALIBAN: I must eat my dinner.   330
    This island's mine, by Sycorax my mother,
    Which thou tak'st from me. When thou camest first
    Thou strok'dst me and made much of me; wouldst give me
    Water with berries in 't; and teach me how
    To name the bigger light, and how the less,
    That burn by day and night. And then I loved thee,
    And showed thee all the qualities o' th' isle,
    The fresh springs, brine-pits, barren place and fertile;
    Cursed be I that did so. All the charms
    Of Sycorax, toads, beetles, bats, light on you.   340
    For I am all the subjects that you have,
    Which first was mine own king. And here you sty me
    In this hard rock, whiles you do keep from me
    The rest o' th' island.

PROSPERO: Thou most lying slave,

63

351– *Abhorred . . . prison.* Some editors give this speech to Prospero, but
62   there seems no convincing ground for making the change.

352   *Which . . . take.* The idea is expressed in *A Midsummer Night's
Dream*, I. i, 49–50, 'You are but as a form in wax By him imprinted'.

353   *Being . . . ill*, being receptive of every kind of evil. *capable*, receptive
particularly to an imprint.

356   *Know . . . meaning*, think clearly.

357   *purposes*, what you intended.

358   *vile*, (*a*) worthless, (*b*) degenerate.

359   *good natures*, i.e. human beings.

363–4 *my . . . curse.* Is this gloating or resentment?

364   *red plague*, one of the kinds of plague sores. *rid*, destroy. The echo
of 'red' stresses the curse.

365–6 *Hag-seed . . . fuel.* Prospero's retort is likewise forceful with
alliteration.

366–7 *and . . . business*, and it were best for you to carry on the other
tasks quickly.

367   *Shrug'st thou.* Throughout the play there is an unusually large
number of stage directions imbedded in the text. *malice*, vicious
thing.

369   *rack*, torture. *old cramps*, (*a*) cramps that afflict old people. See
IV. i, 258 'aged cramps', (*b*) plentiful. See *Macbeth*, II. iii, 2 'have
old turning the key'.

370   *aches.* Pronounced 'aitches'.

370–1 *make . . . din.* Compare Ariel's cries ll. 286–9.

373   *Setebos.* The name comes from R. Eden's *History of Travel*, 1577,
where the Patagonians are described as roaring like bulls and
crying 'upon their great devil Setebos to help them'.

Whom stripes may move, not kindness! I have used thee,
Filth as thou art, with human care, and lodged thee
In mine own cell, till thou didst seek to violate
The honour of my child.

CALIBAN: O ho, O ho, would 't had been done!
Thou didst prevent me; I had peopled else   350
This isle with Calibans.

MIRANDA: Abhorred slave,
Which any print of goodness wilt not take,
Being capable of all ill, I pitied thee,
Took pains to make thee speak, taught thee each hour
One thing or other. When thou didst not, savage,
Know thine own meaning, but wouldst gabble like
A thing most brutish, I endowed thy purposes
With words that made them known. But thy vile race,
Though thou didst learn, had that in 't which good natures
Could not abide to be with; therefore wast thou   360
Deservedly confined into this rock,
Who hadst deserved more than a prison.

CALIBAN: You taught me language, and my profit on 't
Is, I know how to curse. The red plague rid you
For learning me your language.

PROSPERO: Hag-seed, hence!
Fetch us in fuel, and be quick, thou 'rt best,
To answer other business. Shrug'st thou, malice?
If thou neglect'st, or dost unwillingly
What I command, I 'll rack thee with old cramps,
Fill all thy bones with aches, make thee roar,   370
That beasts shall tremble at thy din.

CALIBAN: No, pray thee.
[*Aside*] I must obey, his art is of such power,
It would control my dam's god Setebos,

The Tempest

s.d.   *Exit Caliban.* How does Caliban depart—crawling, slouching, cringing, on all fours?

s.d.   *Enter . . . singing.* Presumably Ariel is in sea-nymph's attire but supposedly invisible (ll. 301-4), and not wearing the usual cloak to represent invisibility. Ariel accompanies his song possibly with a lute. Is he moving rapidly from place to place on the stage or steadily drawing Ferdinand forward? How does Ferdinand move —as in a dream, entranced, cautiously, reluctantly, bewilderedly, rushing hither and thither, gropingly?

     Prospero, motionless, aloof, watching the scene effectively makes the audience aware of his control and power.

377-8   *kissed . . . whist,* (a) kissed the wild waves to silence, or (b) kissed each other, while the wild waves became silent.

379   *Foot it featly,* dance gracefully. Should the sprites be visible to the audience as they dance?

380   *And . . . bear.* Pope's arrangement. *burden,* refrain.

s.d.   *dispersedly,* i.e. from different parts of the stage.

     What is the purpose of this stanza—to draw and console Ferdinand with hints of human dwellings, to suggest security (watch-dogs) and peace (bird of dawning), to signify his entry into the dawn of an enchanted country, to mystify and awe him with a divine presence.

387-8   *It . . . island.* Music was associated with the presence of a god. See *Antony and Cleopatra,* IV. iii, 13-20.

389   *again,* over and over.

391   *Allaying . . . passion.* The power of music to restore harmony or calm storms and human passions is mentioned frequently. See Introduction, pp. 8, 12-13 and *Merchant of Venice,* V. i, 55-88. *passion,* grief.

And make a vassal of him.

PROSPERO: So slave, hence.   [*Exit Caliban*

Enter ARIEL, *invisible, playing and singing;* FERDINAND
following

ARIEL'S *song*

Come unto these yellow sands,
    And then take hands.
Courtsied when you have and kissed
    The wild waves whist.
Foot it featly here and there,
And sweet sprites the burden bear.   380
    Hark, hark!
Burden [*dispersedly*]   Bow-wow.
The watch-dogs bark:
    Burden [*dispersedly*]   Bow-wow.
Hark, hark! I hear
The strain of strutting chanticleer.
Cry, *Burden* [*dispersedly*] Cock-a-diddle-dow.

FERDINAND: Where should this music be? I' th' air or th' earth?
    It sounds no more. And sure it waits upon
    Some god o' th' island. Sitting on a bank,
    Weeping again the King my father's wreck,
    This music crept by me upon the waters,   390
    Allaying both their fury and my passion
    With its sweet air. Thence I have followed it,
    Or it hath drawn me rather. But 'tis gone.
    No, it begins again.

ARIEL *sings*

Full fathom five thy father lies,
    Of his bones are coral made,
Those are pearls that were his eyes;

398– *Nothing . . . strange,* every part of him that will decay undergoes a
400 magical sea-change into some rich and wonderful thing.
      What function has this stanza—to lament the supposed death
      of Alonso, to suggest a kind of consoling transformation to parallel
      the christian baptismal service with its death of the old man and
      birth of the new (see *Henry V,* I. i, 25–7), to prophesy the sea
      change that will befall all of them, to state a theme of meta-
      morphosis?

404 *ditty,* words of a song. *remember,* recall, remind me of.

406 *That . . . owes,* earthly. *owes,* owns. *I . . . me.* Where does Ariel
      go, or are there other instruments playing?

407 *The . . . advance,* raise your eyelids. See IV. i, 177. It has been
      suggested that Prospero's figurative language is that of a magician
      making a spirit visible, or rather removing a charm from some-
      one. What has Miranda been doing from l. 377—sleeping,
      chatting with Prospero, embroidering or spinning, domestic
      duties off-stage?

410 *But,* only that.

414 *that 's beauty's canker,* that eats away and destroys beauty. *canker,*
      maggot.

417– *A . . . noble.* In the platonic mode virtually an admission of love
18 at first sight.
417 *natural,* in nature, earthly.
418– *It . . . it.* The affair develops as my innermost wish would have it
19 do.
420–1 *Most . . . attend.* Miranda thinks Ferdinand a 'thing divine'. He,
      in common with all platonic lovers, regards the lady as a goddess,
      not only because of her beauty but also because he thinks she is
      accompanied, like a goddess, by the mysterious music. In platonic
      thought supreme beauty was by definition divine.
421 *airs,* melodies.
424 *My . . . pronounce,* i.e. my earnest foremost request which I humbly
      place last of all.
425 *O you wonder!* A quibble on Miranda which serves to link the
      two lovers.

    Nothing of him that doth fade
    But doth suffer a sea-change
    Into something rich and strange.   400
    Sea-nymphs hourly ring his knell:

                         Burden. Ding-dong.

    Hark! now I hear them—Ding-dong, bell.
FERDINAND: The ditty does remember my drowned father.
  This is no mortal business, nor no sound
  That the earth owes. I hear it now above me.
PROSPERO: The fringed curtains of thine eye advance,
  And say what thou seest yond.
MIRANDA: What is 't! A spirit?
  Lord, how it looks about. Believe me sir,
  It carries a brave form. But 'tis a spirit.   410
PROSPERO: No wench, it eats and sleeps, and hath such senses
  As we have, such. This gallant which thou seest
  Was in the wreck; and but he 's something stained
  With grief, that 's beauty's canker, thou mightst call him
  A goodly person. He hath lost his fellows,
  And strays about to find 'em.
MIRANDA: I might call him
  A thing divine, for nothing natural
  I ever saw so noble.
PROSPERO: [*Aside*] It goes on I see
  As my soul prompts it. Spirit, fine spirit, I 'll free thee
  Within two days for this.
FERDINAND: Most sure, the goddess   420
  On whom these airs attend. Vouchsafe my prayer
  May know if you remain upon this island,
  And that you will some good instruction give
  How I may bear me here. My prime request,
  Which I do last pronounce, is—O you wonder—
  If you be maid or no?
MIRANDA: No wonder sir,

428–9   *I . . . spoken*. Ferdinand assumes that his father is drowned.

431   *single*, (*a*) solitary, (*b*) sole, (*c*) weak.

432   *He*, i.e. King of Naples whom Ferdinand thinks he is.

434   *never . . . ebb*, i.e. always since that time flooded with tears.

436–7   *the . . . twain*. There is no other indication of this son in the play. Some think that this reference is a remnant from an earlier version of the play, others that Shakespeare was forgetful or changed his plans.

438   *control*, prove you wrong, contradict.

440   *changed eyes*, fallen in love. It was believed that love began through the eyes.

440–1   *Delicate . . . this*. Any response from Ariel?

442   *I . . . wrong*. Is Prospero harsh, stern, sarcastic, polite, ironic?

443–6   *Why . . . way!* Is this an aside, or to whom is Miranda speaking?

446–8   *O . . . Naples*. Ferdinand is so deeply attracted to Miranda that he ignores Prospero.

450,   *light, light*, (*a*) easy, (*b*) little valued.
  451

       Prospero, as Kermode notes, is like the bad-tempered magician of folk story who sets the suitor laborious tasks.

453   *ow'st*, ownest

But certainly a maid.

FERDINAND: My language? Heavens,
I am the best of them that speak this speech,
Were I but where 'tis spoken.

PROSPERO: How? The best?
What wert thou if the King of Naples heard thee?   430

FERDINAND: A single thing, as I am now, that wonders
To hear thee speak of Naples. He does hear me,
And that he does I weep. Myself am Naples,
Who with mine eyes, never since at ebb, beheld
The King my father wrecked.

MIRANDA: Alack, for mercy!

FERDINAND: Yes faith, and all his lords, the Duke of Milan
And his brave son being twain.

PROSPERO: [*Aside*] The Duke of Milan
And his more braver daughter could control thee,
If now 'twere fit to do 't. At the first sight
They have changed eyes. Delicate Ariel,   440
I 'll set thee free for this. A word good sir,
I fear you have done yourself some wrong. A word.

MIRANDA: Why speaks my father so ungently? This
Is the third man that e'er I saw, the first
That e'er I sighed for. Pity move my father
To be inclined my way.

FERDINAND: O, if a virgin,
And your affection not gone forth, I 'll make you
The Queen of Naples.

PROSPERO: Soft sir, one word more.
[*Aside*] They are both in either's powers. But this swift business
I must uneasy make, lest too light winning   450
Make the prize light. One word more. I charge thee
That thou attend me. Thou dost here usurp
The name thou ow'st not, and hast put thyself
Upon this island as a spy, to win it

456   *There's ... temple.* According to the platonic doctrines then
        current physical beauty reflected inner spiritual goodness and
        virtue. The divine attributes of a beautiful body led naturally to
        the imagery of a 'temple', which also had scriptural authority.
        (I *Corinthians*, iii. 17; vi. 19.)

457–8   *If ... with't,* if the Devil were to dwell in so beautiful and virtuous
        a body that good things by their nature would strive to live
        there too, the union of two such incompatibles would be self-
        contradictory. Perhaps a somewhat distorted recollection of the
        words, 'a house divided against itself cannot stand', uttered by
        Christ in refuting the charge that he had cast out a devil by using
        the Devil's powers. (*Matthew*, xii. 22–30; *Mark*, iii. 22–7.)

459   *traitor*, i.e. treacherous.

464   *entertainment*, treatment.

s.d.   By what posture does Ferdinand show that he is charmed from
        moving?

466   *rash*, inconsiderate, hasty. *trial*, judgment.

467   *gentle*, of noble birth and courteously restrains himself in the face
        of your ill-treatment (Mahood). *fearful*, (*a*) cowardly, (*b*) threaten-
        ing.

468   *My ... tutor.* A version of the proverb, 'Do not make the foot the
        head', i.e. do not permit an inferior to rule over his superior and
        so disturb the divinely appointed order of creation.

470   *Come ... ward*, drop your guard.

471–2   *For ... drop.* Prospero uses his staff.

471   *stick.* A belittling word.

479   *To ... men*, by comparison with most men.

From me, the lord on 't.

FERDINAND: No, as I am a man.

MIRANDA: There 's nothing ill can dwell in such a temple:
If the ill spirit have so fair a house,
Good things will strive to dwell with 't.

PROSPERO: Follow me.
Speak not you for him. He's a traitor. Come,
I 'll manacle thy neck and feet together. 460
Sea-water shalt thou drink. Thy food shall be
The fresh-brook mussels, withered roots, and husks
Wherein the acorn cradled. Follow.

FERDINAND: No,
I will resist such entertainment till
Mine enemy has more power.

[*Draws, and is charmed from moving*

MIRANDA: O dear father,
Make not too rash a trial of him, for
He 's gentle, and not fearful.

PROSPERO: What, I say?
My foot my tutor? Put thy sword up traitor;
Who makest a show, but darest not strike; thy conscience
Is so possessed with guilt. Come from thy ward, 470
For I can here disarm thee with this stick,
And make thy weapon drop.

MIRANDA: Beseech you, father.

PROSPERO: Hence! Hang not on my garments.

MIRANDA: Sir have pity.
I 'll be his surety.

PROSPERO: Silence. One word more
Shall make me chide thee, if not hate thee. What,
An advocate for an impostor? Hush.
Thou think'st there is no more such shapes as he,
Having seen but him and Caliban. Foolish wench,
To the most of men this is a Caliban,

483   *nerves*, sinews.

485   *My . . . up*. As in a nightmare, my vital spirits are powerless to transmit the messages to my muscles.

488   *light*, trifling.

490   *corners*. The earth was believed to be three-cornered. See *King John*, V. vi, 116.

491   *liberty*, those who are free.

    How are they disposed on the stage for these final speeches?

496   *by speech*, by his speech. *unwonted*, unusual.

    How do they depart—Ariel by himself, Prospero leading a protesting Miranda from Ferdinand who follows? What happens to Ferdinand's sword?

    This unusually long scene contains the life-histories of Prospero, Miranda, Caliban, and Ariel, and describes the relationships between Prospero and the others. It sums up the past and leads directly into the present.

    It has been claimed that the characters mentioned are symbolic, that Prospero represents the rational soul or Providence, that Miranda represents mercy, Ariel thought, imagination, or the sensitive soul, and Caliban the beast in man or the vegetative soul.

    Do these claims and others like them help to illuminate the play?

And they to him are angels.

MIRANDA: My affections   480
Are then most humble; I have no ambition
To see a goodlier man.

PROSPERO: Come on, obey.
Thy nerves are in their infancy again,
And have no vigour in them.

FERDINAND: So they are.
My spirits, as in a dream, are all bound up.
My father's loss, the weakness which I feel,
The wreck of all my friends, nor this man's threats,
To whom I am subdued, are but light to me,
Might I but through my prison once a day
Behold this maid. All corners else o' th' earth   490
Let liberty make use of. Space enough
Have I in such a prison.

PROSPERO: [*Aside*]   It works.   [*To Ferdinand*] Come on.
[*To Ariel*]   Thou hast done well, fine Ariel!   [*To Ferdinand*]
                                           Follow me.

[*To Ariel*] Hark what thou else shalt do me.

MIRANDA: Be of comfort,
My father 's of a better nature, sir,
Than he appears by speech. This is unwonted
Which now came from him.

PROSPERO: Thou shalt be as free
As mountain winds; but then exactly do
All points of my command.

ARIEL: To th' syllable.

PROSPERO: Come, follow. Speak not for him.   [*Exeunt*   500

Some properties are required—rocks, banks, bushes, etc. In the Banqueting Hall these were probably positioned on the lower stage or even to the sides of the dancing floor immediately before King James.

The distribution of prose and verse in this scene is closely related to the speakers and the immediate situation. See Introduction, pp. 26-9.

Alonso's entry, gait, and movements should indicate his grief and despondency?

1   *Beseech . . . merry.* Any gesture to support the plea?

2-3   *for . . . loss,* our survival far outweighs our losses.

3-4   *Our . . . common,* the event that caused us grief is common enough.

5   *masters . . . merchant,* owners of some merchant vessel.

8   *weigh,* balance.

9-10 *Prithee . . . porridge.* Sebastian repeats 'comfort', and, as Kermode notes, puns on 'peace', porridge at that time being 'pease porridge'. Perhaps there is also an echo of the proverbial expression 'cold comfort'.

         Is this a—sneer, jeer, cynicism, or an attempt to jolly Alonso out of his despair?

11   *visitor,* one who visits the sick or sorrowing to bring them food or 'comfort' ('cold porridge', Dover Wilson).

12-13 *Look . . . strike.* What actions, movements, gestures, facial expressions by Gonzalo prompt this comment?

12   *winding, watch, wit.* The alliteration emphasizes the jeer in the metaphor. *watch.* Perhaps a glance at the meaning 'on the watch for'.

         Gonzalo is obviously racking his brains to find some topic to divert Alonso.

13   *strike,* (*a*) chime (from a watch bell), (*b*) stroke of wit.

15   *tell,* count it. Should Sebastian imitate the sound of the bell?

16   *When . . . offered,* when a person allows his mind to harbour every grief that presents itself.

18   *dollar,* i.e. pay for the 'entertainer'.

19   *Dolour,* grief. A quibble on 'dollar'.

23   *Fie . . . tongue.* Are Antonio and Sebastian attempting—to stop the talk which Alonso resents, to defeat Gonzalo's good intentions, to prevent the restoration of any kind of harmony, to exercise

ACT TWO

SCENE ONE

Enter ALONSO, SEBASTIAN, ANTONIO, GONZALO, ADRIAN, FRANCISCO, *and others*

GONZALO: Beseech you sir, be merry; you have cause—
  So have we all—of joy; for our escape
  Is much beyond our loss. Our hint of woe
  Is common; every day, some sailor's wife,
  The masters of some merchant, and the merchant,
  Have just our theme of woe. But for the miracle—
  I mean our preservation—few in millions
  Can speak like us. Then wisely, good sir, weigh
  Our sorrow with our comfort.

ALONSO: Prithee peace.

SEBASTIAN: He receives comfort like cold porridge.   10

ANTONIO: The visitor will not give him o'er so.

SEBASTIAN: Look, he's winding up the watch of his wit; by and
  by it will strike.

GONZALO: Sir.

SEBASTIAN: One. Tell.

GONZALO: When every grief is entertained that's offered,
  Comes to th' entertainer—

SEBASTIAN: A dollar.

GONZALO: Dolour comes to him indeed, you have spoken truer
  than you purposed.   20

SEBASTIAN: You have taken it wiselier than I meant you should.

GONZALO: Therefore my lord—

ANTONIO: Fie, what a spendthrift is he of his tongue.

77

their malice on Gonzalo? Do their witticisms condemn them or lower Gonzalo in esteem?

29   *old cock.* Is there something in Gonzalo's appearance or speech that makes this apt. Dover Wilson notes lines that associate Gonzalo with birds (ll. 137, 177, 257).

32   *A laughter,* (a) a laugh, (b) a clutch of eggs. However, see *As You Like It*, II. vii, 30–2, 'My lungs began to crow like chanticleer. . . . And I did laugh . . .'? which suggests some association between laughing and crowing. See also *Two Gentlemen of Verona*, II.i, 28 and *Twelfth Night*, I. v, 95.

33   *A match,* agreed!

34   *Though . . . desert.* Is Adrian's style ponderous, slow, affected, twittering (like a chicken)?

35–6   *Ha . . . paid.* Antonio laughs spontaneously, and Sebastian quickly claims that Antonio has had his laughter and the wager is paid. The Folio interchanges the speech headings. Some editors read 'you 've' for 'you 're'. Perhaps Antonio's laugh resembles a cock crow.

40   *miss 't,* i.e. saying 'yet'.

41   *subtle,* fine. *delicate,* pleasant.

42   *temperance,* mild climate.

43   *Temperance.* One of the cardinal Virtues. *delicate,* luxurious, sensuous.

44   *subtle . . . delivered.* Sebastian quibbles on 'subtle', sly, cunning, and 'subtle', delicate, a more learned meaning.

51   *lush and lusty,* thickly grown and vigorous.

53   *eye,* (a) spot, (b) shade, tint. Possibly Sebastian echoes the 'y' of 'tawny'.

       It has been said that the island appears differently to each according to his character. Do you agree? Or is this wilful contradiction?

54   *He . . . much.* Possibly ironic 'he is not much out in his description'.

ALONSO: I prithee spare.

GONZALO: Well, I have done. But yet—

SEBASTIAN: He will be talking.

ANTONIO: Which, of he or Adrian, for a good wager, first begins
to crow?

SEBASTIAN: The old cock.

ANTONIO: The cockerel.   30

SEBASTIAN: Done. The wager?

ANTONIO: A laughter.

SEBASTIAN: A match.

ADRIAN: Though this island seem to be desert—

ANTONIO: Ha, ha, ha!

SEBASTIAN: So, you 're paid.

ADRIAN: Uninhabitable and almost inaccessible—

SEBASTIAN: Yet.

ADRIAN: Yet—

ANTONIO: He could not miss 't.   40

ADRIAN: It must needs be of subtle, tender, and delicate
temperance.

ANTONIO: Temperance was a delicate wench.

SEBASTIAN: Ay, and a subtle; as he most learnedly delivered.

ADRIAN: The air breathes upon us here most sweetly.

SEBASTIAN: As if it had lungs, and rotten ones.

ANTONIO: Or as 't were perfumed by a fen.

GONZALO: Here is everything advantageous to life.

ANTONIO: True; save means to live.

SEBASTIAN: Of that there 's none, or little.   50

GONZALO: How lush and lusty the grass looks! How green!

ANTONIO: The ground indeed is tawny.

SEBASTIAN: With an eye of green in 't.

ANTONIO: He misses not much.

55   *mistake . . . totally.* A quibble on 'misses not much'.

56   *rarity*, wonder.

58   *As . . . are,* as are the wonderful things that travellers maintain are true.

60   *glosses*, brightness.

62–4   *If . . . report.* An allusion to the phrase 'to pocket up wrong' meaning to endure silently an injury, or to swallow one's anger, to conceal the truth. Antonio implies that Gonzalo's pockets are stained. Is this introduced for the sake of Sebastian's quibble?

68–9   *'Twas . . . return.* Ironic.

68   *prosper.* Any glance at Prospero? (See II. ii, 2, 75; III. iii, 99.)

70   *to*, for.

72   *widow Dido's time.* In Virgil's *Æneid* Æneas, escaping from the destruction of Troy in which he lost his wife Creusa, landed at Carthage. Dido, the widow of King Sychaeus, fell in love with him, and the two consummated their love. On Jupiter's command Æneas sailed away secretly, and Dido in despair burnt herself on a funeral pyre.

    As D. C. Allen has noted there was another story of Dido well known in the renaissance. In this she remained a widow after Sychaeus' death, and wooed by many suitors she burnt herself to prevent being forced into marriage. This story was used as a noble example to christian widows. It was available in English in Lydgate's translation of Boccaccio's *De casibus illustrium virorum* and was still topical in 1639 when G. Rivers published *The Heroinæ.*

    Gonzalo is thinking of the latter, Antonio and Sebastian have heard only of the love affair with Æneas which they interpret in the worst sense as the coarse oath implies.

73   *widow,* i.e. that word widow.

82–3   *His . . . too.* According to Ovid Amphion raised the walls of Thebes by playing on his harp. Antonio and Sebastian mockingly

SEBASTIAN: No; he doth but mistake the truth totally.

GONZALO: But the rarity of it is, which is indeed almost beyond credit—

SEBASTIAN: As many vouched rarities are.

GONZALO: That our garments being, as they were, drenched in the sea, hold notwithstanding their freshness and glosses, being rather new-dyed than stained with salt water.   61

ANTONIO: If but one of his pockets could speak, would it not say he lies?

SEBASTIAN: Ay, or very falsely pocket up his report.

GONZALO: Methinks our garments are now as fresh as when we put them on first in Afric, at the marriage of the King's fair daughter Claribel to the King of Tunis.

SEBASTIAN: 'Twas a sweet marriage, and we prosper well in our return.

ADRIAN: Tunis was never graced before with such a paragon to their queen.   71

GONZALO: Not since widow Dido's time.

ANTONIO: Widow? A pox o' that! How came that widow in? Widow Dido!

SEBASTIAN: What if he had said widower Æneas too? Good Lord, how you take it!

ADRIAN: Widow Dido said you? You make me study of that. She was of Carthage, not of Tunis.

GONZALO: This Tunis sir was Carthage.

ADRIAN: Carthage?   80

GONZALO: I assure you Carthage.

ANTONIO: His word is more than the miraculous harp.

SEBASTIAN: He hath raised the wall, and houses too.

ANTONIO: What impossible matter will he make easy next?

remark that Gonzalo has improved on Amphion by identifying
the contemporary Tunis with the ancient Carthage which had
been destroyed.

85–8   *I . . . islands.* Scornful, fantastic absurdity. Editors refer to a
similar passage in *Antony and Cleopatra*, V. ii, 91–2.

89   *I.* Most editors emend to 'Ay' explaining that Gonzalo is affirming
his statement that Tunis was Carthage. The 'I' of the Folio could
be the repeated emphatic 'I' common in Shakespeare. Antonio,
however, deliberately misinterprets it as 'Ay' assuming Gonzalo to
give assent to Antonio's preposterous statement.

91   *Sir.* What has Alonso been doing since l. 24—pacing to and fro,
sitting apart, standing by himself?

95   *Bate*, except.

95–6   *Bate . . . Dido.* Emphatically sarcastic.

98   *sort*, (*a*) fashion, (*b*) word 'sort'.

99   *fished for*, (*a*) arrived at after patient thought, (*b*) rescued after
a long time in the water.

101–2   *You . . . sense*, you thrust these words into my ears against my
wish, as a man who is forcibly fed against his will. Is the image apt?

102   *sense*, i.e. of hearing.

107–8   *what . . . thee?* The Elizabethans frequently refer to a dead person
as food for worms without any sense of incongruity or facetiousness. Is Alonso—petulant, irritable, guilty, conscience-striken, full
of self-pity, weak, maudlin?

108–   *Sir . . . land.* Some assign this speech to Gonzalo as more in
17   keeping with his attempts to comfort Alonso; but this report
coming from Francisco an eye-witness sounds more convincing.

109   *beat . . . him.* A form of back stroke in which the swimmer
pressed downward with his hands and beat the water with his
legs.

115–   *that . . . him*, i.e. the cliff tops leaned over their foot.

16   Is it significant that Ferdinand is the only one—discounting
Stephano's boasts—to show mastery over the sea-storm?

SEBASTIAN: I think he will carry this island home in his pocket, and give it his son for an apple.

ANTONIO: And sowing the kernels of it in the sea, bring forth more islands.

ALONSO: I.

ANTONIO: Why in good time. 90

GONZALO: Sir, we were talking that our garments seem now as fresh as when we were at Tunis at the marriage of your daughter, who is now queen.

ANTONIO: And the rarest that e'er came there.

SEBASTIAN: Bate, I beseech you, widow Dido.

ANTONIO: O, widow Dido? Ay, widow Dido.

GONZALO: Is not sir my doublet as fresh as the first day I wore it? I mean, in a sort.

ANTONIO: That sort was well fished for.

GONZALO: When I wore it at your daughter's marriage? 100

ALONSO: You cram these words into mine ears against
The stomach of my sense. Would I had never
Married my daughter there. For coming thence
My son is lost, and, in my rate, she too,
Who is so far from Italy removed,
I ne'er again shall see her. O thou mine heir
Of Naples and of Milan, what strange fish
Hath made his meal on thee?

FRANCISCO: Sir he may live.
I saw him beat the surges under him,
And ride upon their backs. He trod the water, 110
Whose enmity he flung aside, and breasted
The surge most swollen that met him. His bold head
'Bove the contentious waves he kept, and oared
Himself with his good arms in lusty stroke
To the shore, that o'er his wave-worn basis bowed,
As stooping to relieve him. I not doubt
He came alive to land.

120   *lose*. Some prefer 'loose', but note 'loss' l. 118.

121–2   *Where . . . on't*, in Africa where, to put it mildly, she is completely banished from you, who now have every reason to weep over your great loss.

125–6   *Weighed . . . bow*, and Claribel herself burdened by weighing her dislike of the marriage against her duty to obey her father.

125   *Weighed*, (a) overburdened, (b) balanced.

128   *Moe*, more.

129   *Than . . . them*, i.e. than have survived here. Sebastian assumes that the others of the crew, if not the fleet, have been lost.

       Are Sebastian's remarks to his brother—fraternal, malicious, bullying, showing a habit of blaming others, savage, brutal, an attempt to sting Alonso out of his grief?

130   *dear'st*, most deeply felt.

133   *time*, appropriate time.

135   *most chirurgeonly*, like a good surgeon. A contemptuous reference to Gonzalo's medical advice.

137   *cloudy*, gloomy. *Fowl weather?* The change in spelling suggests a pun of some kind.

138   *plantation*, colony.

139   *He'd . . . mallows*. Antonio and Sebastian take 'plantation' literally = planting, sowing.

142–   *I' . . . people*. Usually held to be closely based on Montaigne's
59   essay 'Of Cannibals', but the general description was traditional.

142–3   *by . . . things*, carry out things in ways opposed to the attitudes

ALONSO: No, no, he 's gone.

SEBASTIAN: Sir you may thank yourself for this great loss,
    That would not bless our Europe with your daughter,
    But rather lose her to an African;   120
    Where she at least is banished from your eye,
    Who hath cause to wet the grief on 't.

ALONSO: Prithee peace.

SEBASTIAN: You were kneeled to, and importuned otherwise
    By all of us. And the fair soul herself
    Weighed between loathness and obedience, at
    Which end o' the beam should bow. We have lost your son,
    I fear for ever. Milan and Naples have
    Moe widows in them of this business' making
    Than we bring men to comfort them.
    The fault 's your own.

ALONSO: So is the dear'st o' th' loss.   130

GONZALO: My lord Sebastian,
    The truth you speak doth lack some gentleness,
    And time to speak it in. You rub the sore,
    When you should bring the plaster.

SEBASTIAN: Very well.

ANTONIO: And most chirurgeonly.

GONZALO: It is foul weather in us all, good sir,
    When you are cloudy.

SEBASTIAN: Fowl weather?

ANTONIO: Very foul.

GONZALO: Had I plantation of this isle my lord—

ANTONIO: He'd sow 't with nettle-seed.

SEBASTIAN: Or docks, or mallows.

GONZALO: And were the king on 't, what would I do?   140

SEBASTIAN: 'Scape being drunk for want of wine.

GONZALO: I' th' commonwealth I would by contraries

85

The Tempest

and methods of civilized life, say what shall not be rather than what shall be.

Is Gonzalo turning the conversation or jibing at Antonio and Sebastian whose opinions have invariably been 'contraries'?

143   *traffic*, trade, commerce.
144   *name*, title.
146   *use of service*, servitude. *succession*, inheritance.
147   *Bourn . . . land*, boundaries. *tilth*, plough land.
148   *No . . . oil.* Montaigne explains that they have been altered by our artificial devices, and diverted from their common order: 'these we have bastardized applying them to the pleasures of our corrupted taste'.
151–3 *Yet . . . beginning.* Is Gonzalo's slip deliberate or due to forgetfulness? See ll. 166–7.

156   *engine*, war machine.

158   *it*, its. *foison*, plenty.

161   *all . . . knaves.* Idleness proverbially begot lust.

163   *golden age.* In classical myth a primal age of plenty and innocence ruled by Saturn. What purposes are served by Gonzalo's description and the comments of Antonio and Sebastian: to give opportunities to the latter to condemn themselves, to ventilate a current topic, to provide irony since the audience has just seen Caliban, to show the impracticability of a society without rule, to challenge Alonso to assert his authority in their present situation?
164   *And . . . sir?* Any movement or gesture from Alonso?
166–7 *minister occasion*, provide with an opportunity.
167   *sensible*, sensitive.

173   *flat-long*, with the flat of the sword, i.e. not a very cutting retort.

86

Execute all things; for no kind of traffic
Would I admit; no name of magistrate:
Letters should not be known; riches, poverty,
And use of service, none: contract, succession,
Bourn, bound of land, tilth, vineyard, none;
No use of metal, corn, or wine, or oil;
No occupation, all men idle, all;
And women too, but innocent and pure.   150
No sovereignty.

SEBASTIAN: Yet he would be king on 't.

ANTONIO: The latter end of his commonwealth forgets the beginning.

GONZALO: All things in common nature should produce
Without sweat or endeavour. Treason, felony,
Sword, pike, knife, gun, or need of any engine,
Would I not have. But nature should bring forth
Of it own kind, all foison, all abundance,
To feed my innocent people.

SEBASTIAN: No marrying 'mong his subjects?   160

ANTONIO: None, man; all idle. Whores and knaves.

GONZALO: I would with such perfection govern sir,
T' excel the golden age.

SEBASTIAN: 'Save his majesty!

ANTONIO: Long live Gonzalo!

GONZALO: And—do you mark me, sir?

ALONSO: Prithee no more. Thou dost talk nothing to me.

GONZALO: I do well believe your Highness, and did it to minister occasion to these gentlemen, who are of such sensible and nimble lungs that they always use to laugh at nothing.

ANTONIO: 'T was you we laughed at.

GONZALO: Who in this kind of merry fooling am nothing to you. So you may continue and laugh at nothing still.   171

ANTONIO: What a blow was there given.

SEBASTIAN: An it had not fallen flat-long.

The Tempest

174–6 *you . . . changing.* Kermode notes that Gonzalo may be alluding to the proverb, 'When the moon's in the full then wit's in the wane'. Gonzalo is obviously angry (ll. 169–71) and sarcastically suggests that their wits would be so weak that they would attempt the ridiculously impossible feat. Perhaps a retort for ll. 84–8.

175 *sphere*, orbit.

177 *go a bat-fowling*, (a) bird-catching, (b) tricking the weak-witted i.e. Gonzalo. On moonless nights men carrying torches disturbed bush-roosting birds which, fluttering at the lights were knocked down by 'bats', or staves with bushy twigs.

179– *I . . . weakly*, I will not risk losing my good judgment over so
80 slight a matter.

180 *laugh me asleep.* Dover Wilson suggests a pun on 'luff asleep', to draw a ship into the wind to stop it, and adds that 'heavy' = going blow (of a ship). This seems strained. Perhaps Gonzalo is sarcastically inviting them to continue aiming their feeble witticisms at him until he falls asleep out of sheer boredom. *heavy*, sleepy. Gonzalo attributes his sleepiness to their conversation, not to the music which apparently is heard only by the audience.

181 *Go . . . us.* How do they arrange themselves?

183 *with themselves*, as they close their lids.

184–9 *Please . . . safety.* Are Sebastian and Antonio—considerate, dutiful, loyal, underhand, opportunists, treacherous, sinister?

185 *omit*, neglect. Do not fail to take advantage of this sleep which now offers itself.

193 *I . . . nimble.* Perhaps the failure of Ariel's music to send these two to sleep is intended to show their treachery:

> The man that hath no music in himself,
> Nor is not moved with concord of sweet sounds,
> Is fit for treasons, stratagems, and spoils;
> Let no such man be trusted . . . .
>
> *Merchant of Venice*, V. i, 83–6.

spirits are nimble, faculties are active.

194 *as by consent*, with one accord.

198 *The . . . thee*, circumstances prompt you to seize your opportunity.

88

GONZALO: You are gentlemen of brave mettle; you would lift
the moon out of her sphere, if she would continue in it five
weeks without changing.

Enter ARIEL, *invisible, playing solemn music*

SEBASTIAN: We would so, and then go a bat-fowling.

ANTONIO: Nay good my lord, be not angry.

GONZALO: No I warrant you, I will not adventure my discretion
so weakly. Will you laugh me asleep, for I am very heavy?

ANTONIO: Go sleep, and hear us. 181
                    [*All sleep except Alonso, Sebastian, and Antonio*

ALONSO: What, all so soon asleep? I wish mine eyes
Would, with themselves, shut up my thoughts. I find
They are inclined to do so.

SEBASTIAN: Please you sir,
Do not omit the heavy offer of it.
It seldom visits sorrow; when it doth,
It is a comforter.

ANTONIO: We two, my lord,
Will guard your person while you take your rest,
And watch your safety.

ALONSO: Thank you. Wondrous heavy.
                    [*Alonso sleeps. Exit Ariel*

SEBASTIAN: What a strange drowsiness possesses them. 190

ANTONIO: It is the quality o' th' climate.

SEBASTIAN: Why
Doth it not then our eyelids sink? I find not
Myself disposed to sleep.

ANTONIO: Nor I, my spirits are nimble.
They fell together all, as by consent;
They dropp'd, as by a thunder-stroke. What might,
Worthy Sebastian? O, what might? No more.
And yet methinks I see it in thy face,
What thou shouldst be. The occasion speaks thee, and

199   *My . . . sees*, my imagination sees with firm certainty.
199–   *crown . . . head.* The emblem picture of Ambition (Ripa, *Icono-*
200   *logia*) depicts a crown descending on his head.

202–3   *It . . . sleep*, i.e. it is the fantastic speech that people utter while
        asleep, and you are speaking in your sleep. Sebastian is cautious.

207–8   *Thou . . . waking.* Antonio skilfully uses Sebastian's 'sleep'—
        'waking' imagery, inverting his last thought 'standing . . .
        asleep' to give force to his own argument.
208–9   *Thou . . . snores.* Sebastian jests, refusing to take Antonio seriously.
        distinctly, articulately, intelligibly.

212   *Trebles thee o'er*, makes you thrice the man you are. Sisson suggests
        that the metaphor is from the game of draughts: 'At a stroke
        Sebastian will overleap three superiors, Antonio, Ferdinand and
        Alonso, and become King in one move'. *standing water*, a short
        period at high or low water during which there is no rise or fall.
213   *flow*, i.e. rise on the flood tide of fortune.
214   *Hereditary sloth*, (*a*) natural laziness, (*b*) the fault of having been
        born younger than my brother, Alonso (Kermode).
215–   *If . . . it*, if only you realized how the phrasing 'hereditary sloth'
   17   of your flippant remark adds point to my proposal.
216   *stripping*, deriding.
217   *invest.* Perhaps a hint at a royal investiture.
218   *do . . . run*, i.e. their fortunes touch rock bottom. See *Antony and
        Cleopatra*, I. iv, 43; *Julius Cæsar*, IV. iii, 218–21.
220   *setting . . . cheek*, the look in your eye and the expression on your
        face.
221   *matter*, some serious matter.
222   *throes thee much*, costs you much labour and effort.

My strong imagination sees a crown
Dropping upon thy head.

SEBASTIAN: What, art thou waking?   200

ANTONIO: Do you not hear me speak?

SEBASTIAN: I do, and surely
It is a sleepy language, and thou speak'st
Out of thy sleep. What is it thou didst say?
This is a strange repose, to be asleep
With eyes wide open; standing, speaking, moving,
And yet so fast asleep.

ANTONIO: Noble Sebastian,
Thou let'st thy fortune sleep—die, rather; wink'st
Whiles thou art waking.

SEBASTIAN: Thou dost snore distinctly,
There 's meaning in thy snores.

ANTONIO: I am more serious than my custom. You   210
Must be so too, if heed me; which to do
Trebles thee o'er.

SEBASTIAN: Well, I am standing water.

ANTONIO: I 'll teach you how to flow.

SEBASTIAN: Do so. To ebb
Hereditary sloth instructs me.

ANTONIO: O,
If you but knew how you the purpose cherish
Whiles thus you mock it; how in stripping it,
You more invest it. Ebbing men indeed
Most often do so near the bottom run
By their own fear or sloth.

SEBASTIAN: Prithee say on.
The setting of thine eye and cheek proclaim   220
A matter from thee, and a birth, indeed,
Which throes thee much to yield.

ANTONIO: Thus sir.

223   *this . . . remembrance*, i.e. Gonzalo, whose memory fails him (l.
       152–3).

224–5 *Who . . . earthed*, i.e. who will be as little remembered when he is
       buried as he remembers things now.

226–7 *For . . . persuade*, i.e. Gonzalo's duty as a councillor.
       Antonio implies that Gonzalo's function makes him fly in the
       face of facts.

230   *out . . . hope*. Again Antonio plays on Sebastian's words to support
       his case.

237–   *She . . . discharge*. Antonio seeks by inflated comparisons delivered
45   with force to convince Sebastian that he is closest to the throne
       of Milan. How should Antonio position himself as he intensifies
       his persuasions?

238   *Ten . . . life*, i.e. a lifetime is not long enough to reach her.

239   *note*, knowledge, news. *post*, messenger.

241   *from*, coming from.

243–5 *And . . . discharge*. Ironical in view of Prospero's words (I. ii,
       178–84) Kermode notes the theatrical puns 'perform', 'act',
       'prologue', 'discharge'.

245   *stuff*, hyperbole, exaggerated nonsense.

247–8 *'twixt . . . space*. A deflating understatement.

248   *cubit*, about 20 inches.

Although this lord of weak remembrance, this,
Who shall be of as little memory
When he is earthed, hath here almost persuaded—
For he 's a spirit of persuasion, only
Professes to persuade—the King his son 's alive,
'T is as impossible that he's undrowned,
As he that sleeps here swims.

SEBASTIAN: I have no hope
That he 's undrowned.

ANTONIO: O, out of that no hope   230
What great hope have you? No hope that way is
Another way so high a hope that even
Ambition cannot pierce a wink beyond,
But doubt discovery there. Will you grant with me
That Ferdinand is drowned?

SEBASTIAN: He 's gone.

ANTONIO: Then tell me,
Who 's the next heir of Naples?

SEBASTIAN: Claribel.

ANTONIO: She that is queen of Tunis; she that dwells
Ten leagues beyond man's life; she that from Naples
Can have no note, unless the sun were post—
The man i' th' moon 's too slow—till new-born chins   240
Be rough and razorable; she that—from whom
We all were sea-swallow'd, though some cast again,
And by that destiny to perform an act
Whereof what 's past is prologue, what to come
In yours and my discharge.

SEBASTIAN: What stuff is this? How say you?
'Tis true, my brother's daughter 's queen of Tunis;
So is she heir of Naples; 'twixt which regions
There is some space.

ANTONIO: A space whose every cubit
Seems to cry out, 'How shall that Claribel

93

The Tempest

250   *Measure*, travel over. *Keep*, i.e. Claribel.

251   *Wake*, awake to his opportunity.

251-3   *Say . . . are.* Sleep was frequently described as death's image or counterfeit.

252-3   *why . . . are*, i.e. powerless and functionless.

254   *prate*, talk.

256-7   *I . . . chat.* I myself could talk as profoundly. *chough.* Possibly here a rook, or a jackdaw as in *A Midsummer Night's Dream*, III. ii, 21. *chat*, echoic of the bird's chattering cries.

260-1   *content . . . fortune.* Ironic. Perhaps a glance at the proverb, 'content is worth a crown'.

261   *Tender*, (*a*) regard, (*b*) be consistent with.

263-4   *And . . . before.* The image of the usurper wearing the garments he has achieved occurs elsewhere in Shakespeare. *Macbeth*, I. iii, 108-109; V. ii, 20-1.

264   *feater*, more gracefully.

265   *fellows*, equals, companions.

266   *But . . . conscience*, either, 'except for your conscience', or, 'what of your conscience?'

267-8   *if . . . slipper*, if it were as troublesome as a blister, I would merely wear a slipper.

267   *kibe*, a chilblain, blister.

269   *deity . . . bosom*, i.e. that rules my heart.

270-1   *candied . . . molest.* Perhaps 'may their bitterness be turned to sweetness and dissolved before they interfere'.

273   *If . . . dead.* See note ll. 251-3.

276   *perpetual . . . aye.* Cynically flippant.

277   *morsel.* Shakespeare occasionally associates the word with death (? Latin, *mors*) *King John*, IV. iii, 143; *Romeo and Juliet*, V. iii, 46; *Antony and Cleopatra*, III. xiii, 116.

279   *suggestion.* Sinister understatement.

280   *tell the clock*, i.e. become time-servers, vicars of Bray.

Measure us back to Naples? Keep in Tunis,   250
And let Sebastian wake.' Say, this were death
That now hath seized them; why they were no worse
Than now they are. There be that can rule Naples
As well as he that sleeps; lords that can prate
As amply and unnecessarily
As this Gonzalo. I myself could make
A chough of as deep chat. O, that you bore
The mind that I do, what a sleep were this
For your advancement. Do you understand me?

SEBASTIAN: Methinks I do.

ANTONIO: And how does your content   260
Tender your own good fortune?

SEBASTIAN: I remember
You did supplant your brother Prospero.

ANTONIO: True:
And look how well my garments sit upon me,
Much feater than before. My brother's servants
Were then my fellows, now they are my men.

SEBASTIAN: But for your conscience?

ANTONIO: Ay sir, where lies that? If 'twere a kibe,
'Twould put me to my slipper. But I feel not
This deity in my bosom. Twenty consciences
That stand 'twixt me and Milan, candied be they,   270
And melt ere they molest. Here lies your brother,
No better than the earth he lies upon,
If he were that which now he's like—that's dead—
Whom I with this obedient steel, three inches of it,
Can lay to bed for ever; whiles you doing thus,
To the perpetual wink for aye might put
This ancient morsel, this Sir Prudence, who
Should not upbraid our course. For all the rest,
They'll take suggestion as a cat laps milk;
They'll tell the clock to any business that   280

281   *case*, i.e. legal case.

284   *tribute*. Any movement or gesture to underline Sebastian's decision? There is a hideous evil in this plot since it is not only fratricidal, the curse of Cain, but it is pointless since, as far as Antonio and Sebastian know, return to Milan is improbable.

289–   *That . . . living*. Ariel first addresses the sleeping Gonzalo and then
  90 explains his mission to the audience. Is he accompanying himself, or are musicians placed elsewhere?

290   *project*. See V. i, 1.

292   *Open-eyed conspiracy*, i.e. (*a*) by those who are awake, (*b*) watchful for opportunities. The emblem figure Conspiracy had eyes woven into his cloak.

297   *sudden*, quick.

297–8 *Now . . . King!* Gonzalo shakes the King.

300   *ghastly looking*. Because they have been surprised, or because they are about to commit murder?

301   *securing your repose*. Telling irony after ll. 271–7.

302   *hollow*, resounding, echoing, sepulchral, dismal.

We say befits the hour.

SEBASTIAN: Thy case, dear friend,
Shall be my precedent. As thou got'st Milan,
I'll come by Naples. Draw thy sword; one stroke
Shall free thee from the tribute which thou pay'st,
And I the king shall love thee.

ANTONIO: Draw together,
And when I rear my hand, do you the like
To fall it on Gonzalo.

SEBASTIAN: O, but one word.   [*They talk apart*

Enter ARIEL, *invisible, with music and song*

ARIEL: My master through his art foresees the danger
That you, his friend, are in; and sends me forth—
For else his project dies—to keep them living.   290
                      [*Sings in Gonzalo's ear*
            While you here do snoring lie,
            Open-eyed conspiracy
               His time doth take.
            If of life you keep a care,
            Shake off slumber, and beware.
               Awake, awake!

ANTONIO: Then let us both be sudden.

GONZALO: *Wakes.*   Now, good angels
Preserve the King.   [*They wake*

ALONSO: Why, how now? Ho, awake! Why are you drawn?
Wherefore this ghastly looking?

GONZALO: What's the matter?   300

SEBASTIAN: Whiles we stood here securing your repose,
Even now, we heard a hollow burst of bellowing
Like bulls, or rather lions. Did't not wake you?
It struck mine ear most terribly.

ALONSO: I heard nothing.

ANTONIO: O, 'twas a din to fright a monster's ear,

308   *humming*. See III. ii, 131.

316   *Lead away*. Do they depart—in twos and threes, in different directions, together for safety; stealthily, cautiously, furtively, suspiciously, fearfully?

       Is the value of this scene—to display Prospero's vigilance and power, to reveal the unprincipled nature of Antonio and Sebastian, to demonstrate the uprise of evil when order is destroyed, to justify Prospero's action and later to confirm the magnanimity of his forgiveness?

The Island

S.D.   Caliban's movements should suggest his truculent, resentful mood. For his use of verse in this scene and later see Introduction, pp. 26-9.

1-3   *All . . . disease*. Many diseases were thought to rise in vapour from stagnant places.

2   *flats*, muddy tidal land, swamps.

3   *By inch-meal*, inch by inch. *His . . . me*. Does this mean 'I am always overheard', or is it caused by a clap of thunder? Does Caliban cower or stand defiantly?

5   *urchin-shows*, ghostly goblins.

6   *firebrand*, torch. Ariel 'flamed amazement' (I. ii, 198).

9   *mow*, pull faces, grimace.

       Editors refer to Harsnet, *Declaration of Popish Impostures* (1603) which Shakespeare drew on in *King Lear*: 'They make antic faces, girn, mow and mop like an ape, tumble like a hedge-hog'.

98

To make an earthquake; sure it was the roar
Of a whole herd of lions.
ALONSO: Heard you this, Gonzalo?
GONZALO: Upon mine honour, sir, I heard a humming,
    And that a strange one too, which did awake me.
    I shaked you sir, and cried. As mine eyes opened,   310
    I saw their weapons drawn. There was a noise,
    That's verily. 'T is best we stand upon our guard,
    Or that we quit this place. Let's draw our weapons.
ALONSO: Lead off this ground, and let's make further search
    For my poor son.
GONZALO: Heavens keep him from these beasts.
    For he is sure i' th' island.
ALONSO: Lead away.
ARIEL: Prospero my lord shall know what I have done.
    So, King, go safely on to seek thy son.   [*Exeunt*

SCENE TWO

Enter CALIBAN *with a burden of wood. A noise of thunder
heard*

CALIBAN: All the infections that the sun sucks up
    From bogs, fens, flats, on Prosper fall, and make him
    By inch-meal a disease. His spirits hear me,
    And yet I needs must curse. But they 'll nor pinch,
    Fright me with urchin-shows, pitch me i' th' mire,
    Nor lead me, like a firebrand, in the dark
    Out of my way, unless he bid 'em; but
    For every trifle are they set upon me;
    Sometime like apes, that mow and chatter at me,
    And after bite me, then like hedgehogs, which   10
    Lie tumbling in my barefoot way, and mount

13 *wound*, coiled round.
    What kind of entry is appropriate for Trinculo who is described in the list of characters as a jester—fearful, bewildered, perky, miserable? His costume is probably the fool's long motley gaberdine.

18 *Here's . . . shrub.* No scenery of shrubs and bushes. *bear off*, protect against.

21 *bombard*, (*a*) cannon, (*b*) large leather wine vessel.

23 *What . . . here?* What actions are appropriate?
    In this scene and elsewhere in the play numerous stage directions are both explicit and implicit in the text.

24 *A . . . fish.* See V. i, 265–6.

25 *of,* The comma perhaps indicates a pause to waft away the odour, or to search for the right phrase to describe it.

26 *poor-john*, dried hake. *A strange fish.* This starts the train of thought of the freak-show and the topical hit at England.

27 *painted*, usually explained as a painting displayed on a board outside a fair booth. Alternatively perhaps the fish was stuffed, varnished, and touched up to amaze the credulous.

28–9 *monster . . . man*, (*a*) makes a man's fortune, (*b*) a paradox stressed by the quibble on the pronunciation 'mon' for 'man'. See *A Midsummer Night's Dream*, III. ii, 348–9.

29 *Any . . . man*, a further pun on 'makes'. (*a*) makes a fortune, (*b*) is equivalent to, passes for.

30 *doit*, a very small coin.

31 *dead Indian.* Many of the Indians who were brought to England died from the diseases common in European cities.

31–2 *Legged . . . troth.* What actions are appropriate?

32 *Warm*, i.e. a fish would be cold.

33 *suffered*, suffered death.

35 *gaberdine*, smock, cloak.

37 *shroud*, cover myself, shelter. *dregs*, i.e. of the 'bombard'.

s.D. Stephano is merry rather than drunk.

Their pricks at my footfall. Sometime am I
All wound with adders, who with cloven tongues
Do hiss me into madness.

Enter TRINCULO

Lo, now lo,

Here comes a spirit of his, and to torment me
For bringing wood in slowly. I 'll fall flat,
Perchance he will not mind me.   17

TRINCULO: Here 's neither bush nor shrub to bear off any
weather at all, and another storm brewing; I hear it sing i'
th' wind. Yond same black cloud, yond huge one, looks like a
foul bombard that would shed his liquor. If it should thunder
as it did before, I know not where to hide my head. Yond same
cloud cannot choose but fall by pailfuls. What have we here?
A man or a fish? Dead or alive? A fish: he smells like a fish. A
very ancient and fish-like smell. A kind of not of, the newest
poor-john. A strange fish. Were I in England now, as once I
was, and had but this fish painted, not a holiday fool there but
would give a piece of silver. There would this monster make a
man. Any strange beast there makes a man. When they will
not give a doit to relieve a lame beggar, they will lay out ten
to see a dead Indian. Legged like a man. And his fins like arms.
Warm, o' my troth. I do now let loose my opinion, hold it no
longer, this is no fish, but an islander, that hath lately suffered
by a thunderbolt. [*Thunder.*] Alas, the storm is come again.
My best way is to creep under his gaberdine; there is no other
shelter hereabout. Misery acquaints a man with strange bed-
fellows. I will here shroud till the dregs of the storm be
past.   38

Enter STEPHANO, singing: a bottle in his hand

STEPHANO: I shall no more to sea, to sea,

Here shall I die ashore—

This is a very scurvy tune to sing at a man's funeral. Well,
here 's my comfort.   [*Drinks*

43   *swabber*, one who washed the decks and cleaned the ship.

47   *tang*, (*a*) sharp edge, (*b*) twang. Perhaps a play on 'tongue' and 'tang' (pronounced 'tong').

        Stephano's ribald song fixes his character. It is one of the evil roundelays whereby music could corrupt.

53   *Do . . . me*. Trinculo is restless. See ll. 74–5.

54–5   *Do . . . Ind*. Perhaps an allusion to the proverb, 'There's no putting of tricks on old travellers' i.e. don't attempt to deceive me by conjuring tricks.

55   *savages*, i.e. the 'wild men', 'woodwoses' of renaissance and contemporary pageants and art.

57–8   *as . . . ground*. Stephano changes the 'two legs' of the proverb to 'four legs' in view of the strange composite creature (Trinculo and Caliban).

62   *ague*, fever. Both Caliban and Trinculo are shaking.

64   *recover*, revive, restore.

65   *for*, fit for.

65–6   *that . . . leather*, i.e. as fine an emperor as could be. See ll. 57.

66   *neat's leather*, cowhide.

69   *fit*, seizure by a spirit.

72   *I . . . him*, i.e. no price will be too high for him.

75   *trembling*. Trembling was supposed to be a sign of possession by a spirit. Trinculo is quaking with fright. *works upon*, Prospero's magic power is at work in you.

[*Sings.*

> The master, the swabber, the boatswain, and I,
> > The gunner, and his mate
> Loved Mall, Meg, and Marian, and Margery,
> > But none of us cared for Kate.
> > For she had a tongue with a tang,
> > Would cry to a sailor, Go hang!
> She loved not the savour of tar nor of pitch,   49
> > Yet a tailor might scratch her where'er she did itch.
> > Then to sea, boys, and let her go hang

This is a scurvy tune too; but here 's my comfort.   [*Drinks*

CALIBAN: Do not torment me, O!

STEPHANO: What 's the matter? Have we devils here? Do you put tricks upon 's with savages, and men of Ind ha? I have not 'scaped drowning to be afeard now of your four legs. For it hath been said, as proper a man as ever went on four legs cannot make him give ground. And it shall be said so again while Stephano breathes at' nostrils.

CALIBAN: The spirit torments me. Oh!   60

STEPHANO: This is some monster of the isle with four legs, who hath got, as I take it, an ague. Where the devil should he learn our language? I will give him some relief, if it be but for that. If I can recover him, and keep him tame, and get to Naples with him, he 's a present for any emperor that ever trod on neat's leather.

CALIBAN: Do not torment me prithee. I 'll bring my wood home faster.   68

STEPHANO: He 's in his fit now, and does not talk after the wisest. He shall taste of my bottle. If he have never drunk wine afore, it will go near to remove his fit. If I can recover him, and keep him tame, I will not take too much for him; he shall pay for him that hath him, and that soundly.

CALIBAN: Thou dost me yet but little hurt; thou wilt anon, I know it by thy trembling. Now Prosper works upon thee.

76–7   *Here . . . cat.* Proverbially good liquor made even cats speak.

79   *You . . . friend*, you won't seem to realize that I'm your friend.
        chaps, jaws.

82   *delicate*, exquisite, wonderful.

86   *Amen*, stop, that's enough.

88–90   *Mercy . . . spoon.* Does Stephano kneel, raise his hands in supplica-
        tion, jump away?
89–90   *I . . . spoon.* Proverbially he who supped with the Devil needed a
        long spoon to keep out of harm's way.

96   *siege*, droppings, excrement.
97   *moon-calf*, misshapen creature. It was thought that the influence of
        the moon could cause deformity before birth.
98–9   *But . . . drowned*, i.e. that he is alive and not a ghost.

103–4   *Prithee . . . constant.* Is Trinculo turning Stephano round and feel-
        ing him to make sure that he is alive or dancing him round in
        joy? *my . . . constant.* Too much liquor, or is he seasick?

108–   *How . . . hid.* What is Caliban doing during these lines?
22
109   *swear . . . hither.* Perhaps to make sure that Trinculo is not a ghost.

STEPHANO: Come on your ways. Open your mouth. Here is
that which will give language to you, cat. Open your mouth;
this will shake your shaking, I can tell you, and that soundly.
You cannot tell who's your friend. Open your chaps again.

TRINCULO: I should know that voice. It should be—but he is
drowned; and these are devils. O defend me!   81

STEPHANO: Four legs and two voices—a most delicate monster.
His forward voice now is to speak well of his friend; his backward voice is to utter foul speeches, and to detract. If all the
wine in my bottle will recover him, I will help his ague. Come.
Amen, I will pour some in thy other mouth.

TRINCULO: Stephano.

STEPHANO: Doth thy other mouth call me? Mercy, mercy! This
is a devil, and no monster: I will leave him, I have no long
spoon.   90

TRINCULO: Stephano. If thou beest Stephano, touch me, and
speak to me; for I am Trinculo—be not afeard—thy good
friend Trinculo.

STEPHANO: If thou beest Trinculo, come forth. I'll pull thee by
the lesser legs. If any be Trinculo's legs, these are they. Thou
art very Trinculo indeed. How camest thou to be the siege of
this moon-calf? Can he vent Trinculos?

TRINCULO: I took him to be killed with a thunder-stroke. But
art thou not drowned Stephano? I hope now thou art not
drowned. Is the storm overblown? I hid me under the dead
moon-calf's gaberdine for fear of the storm. And art thou
living Stephano? O Stephano, two Neapolitans 'scaped!

STEPHANO: Prithee do not turn me about, my stomach is not
constant.   104

CALIBAN: These be fine things, an if they be not sprites.
That's a brave god, and bears celestial liquor.
I will kneel to him.

STEPHANO: How didst thou 'scape? How camest thou hither?
swear by this bottle how thou camest hither. I escaped upon

118   *kiss the book.* Stephano takes Trinculo's 'I'll be sworn' literally.
      book, i.e. bottle.
119   *made . . . goose.* Does Trinculo's appearance suggest this? There
      may be a pun on 'made', 'mad' with either a glance at the wild-
      goose's alleged stupidity, or at Trinculo's, the giddy goose, who
      keeps whirling round Stephano.

126   *when time was,* once upon a time.
127–8 *and . . . bush.* It was believed that the markings on the moon's
      surface represented a man with a lantern, a bush of thorns, and a
      dog.
128   *My . . . thee.* See I. ii, 335–6.
130   *anon,* soon.
131   *shallow,* brainless.
132   *weak,* (*a*) feeble, (*b*) credulous.
133   *drawn,* drunk.

137   *perfidious.* Travellers often reported that natives while hospitable
      were sometimes not to be trusted.

142–3 *I . . . him,* i.e. to prove his courage which has not been noteworthy.

a butt of sack, which the sailors heaved o'erboard, by this
bottle which I made of the bark of a tree with mine own hands,
since I was cast ashore. 112

CALIBAN: I 'll swear upon that bottle, to be thy true subject, for
the liquor is not earthly.

STEPHANO: Here. Swear then how thou escapedst.

TRINCULO: Swum ashore, man, like a duck. I can swim like a
duck, I 'll be sworn.

STEPHANO: Here, kiss the book. Though thou canst swim like
a duck, thou art made like a goose.

TRINCULO: O Stephano, hast any more of this? 120

STEPHANO: The whole butt, man; my cellar is in a rock by the
sea-side, where my wine is hid. How now moon-calf, how
does thine ague?

CALIBAN: Hast thou not dropped from heaven?

STEPHANO: Out o' th' moon, I do assure thee. I was the man i'
th' moon when time was.

CALIBAN: I have seen thee in her, and I do adore thee.
My mistress showed me thee, and thy dog, and thy bush.

STEPHANO: Come, swear to that. Kiss the book. I will furnish it
anon with new contents. Swear. 130

TRINCULO: By this good light, this is a very shallow monster. I
afeard of him? A very weak monster. The man i' th' moon.
A most poor credulous monster. Well drawn monster, in
good sooth.

CALIBAN: I 'll show thee every fertile inch o' th' island.
And I will kiss thy foot. I prithee be my god.

TRINCULO: By this light, a most perfidious and drunken
monster. When 's god 's asleep, he 'll rob his bottle.

CALIBAN: I 'll kiss thy foot. I 'll swear myself thy subject.

STEPHANO: Come on then. Down, and swear. 140

TRINCULO: I shall laugh myself to death at this puppy-headed
monster. A most scurvy monster. I could find in my heart to
beat him—

145   *But that.* Trinculo finishes his sentence.

145-6 *An abominable monster.* Is this a comment on Caliban's grovelling, slobbering, smell, or as Dover Wilson suggests his rear view when kneeling?

147-   *I'll ... man.* The wine has loosened Caliban's tongue.
  51

155   *pig-nuts*, earth-nuts.

157   *marmoset*, i.e. for food.

159   *Young scamels.* Variously interpreted, but 'scamel', 'godwit' seems most likely. This bird was a very great delicacy and easily caught as its young were very tame.

162   *we.* The royal 'we'. *inherit*, take the sovereignty. *bear my bottle.* Spoken to Trinculo.

169   *trenchering*, trenchers.

170   *'Ban, 'Ban, Cacaliban.* A drunken and hiccoughy effort.

171   *Get ... man.* Is this a shout of defiance at Prospero, or a cry of joy at feeling himself a new man?

172   *freedom.* Ironic comment on service under the drunken Stephano. *high-day*, a day for celebration.

174   *O ... way.* A mock royal procession.

STEPHANO: Come, kiss.

TRINCULO: But that the poor monster's in drink. An abominable monster.

CALIBAN: I'll show thee the best springs. I'll pluck thee berries.
I'll fish for thee, and get thee wood enough.
A plague upon the tyrant that I serve;
I'll bear him no more sticks, but follow thee,   150
Thou wondrous man.

TRINCULO: A most ridiculous monster, to make a wonder of
a poor drunkard.

CALIBAN: I prithee let me bring thee where crabs grow;
And I with my long nails will dig thee pig-nuts;
Show thee a jay's nest, and instruct thee how
To snare the nimble marmoset. I'll bring thee
To clustering filberts, and sometimes I'll get thee
Young scamels from the rock. Wilt thou go with me?   159

STEPHANO: I prithee now lead the way without any more
talking. Trinculo, the King and all our company else being
drowned, we will inherit here. Here, bear my bottle. Fellow
Trinculo, we'll fill him by and by again.

CALIBAN: [*Sings drunkenly*]
            Farewell master; farewell, farewell.

TRINCULO: A howling monster; a drunken monster.

CALIBAN: No more dams I'll make for fish,
                    Nor fetch in firing
                    At requiring;
                Nor scrape trenchering, nor wash dish.
                    'Ban, 'Ban, Cacaliban   170
                    Has a new master. Get a new man.
    Freedom, high-day, high-day, freedom, freedom, high-day,
    freedom!

STEPHANO: O brave monster. Lead the way.   [*Exeunt*

S.D.   Is Ferdinand brisk, weary, strong, despondent, active, leisured? Is the pile of logs on the stage or not?

1–2   *There . . . off*, Some enjoyable pastimes are full of toil which is counterbalanced by the pleasure they give.

2   *baseness*, humble undertakings, menial tasks.

3   *nobly undergone*, undertaken for noble ends.

3–4   *most . . . ends.* Perhaps proverbial, 'A hard beginning makes a good ending', or even a reminiscence of *2 Corinthians*, vi. 10, 'as poor, yet making many rich'.

5   *as . . . odious*, as grievous as it is hateful.

6   *quickens*, gives life to. *dead*, purposeless.

11   *Upon . . . injunction*, under the threat of harsh punishment.

12–13   *such . . . executor*, such a servile task never had so noble a person to carry it out.

13   *I forget*, i.e. to do my work.

15   *Most . . . it.* One of the most famous of cruxes. The Folio reading is retained here although it is difficult to interpret it. The many emendations fall into three groups: (*a*) busy-idlest or busy when idlest; (*b*) busy-liest or busilest; (*c*) busy, least. The first presupposes a compositor who dropped his type and a version of the proverb 'never less alone than when alone' type. The second assumes a wrong division of an unfamiliar word and the analogy of 'easilest' in *Cymbeline*, IV. ii, 207. The third assumes a misplaced comma. None is convincing. As emendation seems necessary I suggest 'busy else'. The Folio 'lest' resulted from an interplacing of 'e' and 'l' and a misreading of 'e' for 't'.

The organization of thought in these fifteen lines is very like that of a Shakespearean sonnet—an apt introduction to a love scene. See *Romeo and Juliet*, I. v, 91–104.

Ferdinand's log-carrying is a typical fairy-tale situation. What is being tested? Contrast Caliban's attitude. What value have the paradoxes and antitheses—to justify Ferdinand's submission, to show his nobility through service, to show the intensity of his love?

S.D.   Prospero enters possibly on the balcony or even back stage. In the Banqueting Hall he would be on the raised back-stage.

18–19   *When . . . you*, i.e. the oozings of sap or gum from burning logs.

Is this image—over-fanciful, elegantly associative, witty, **consolatory**, decorous?

ACT THREE

SCENE ONE

Enter FERDINAND, *bearing a log*

FERDINAND : There be some sports are painful, and their labour
Delight in them sets off. Some kinds of baseness
Are nobly undergone, and most poor matters
Point to rich ends. This my mean task
Would be as heavy to me as odious, but
The mistress which I serve quickens what's dead,
And makes my labours pleasures. O she is
Ten times more gentle than her father's crabbed,
And he 's composed of harshness. I must remove
Some thousands of these logs, and pile them up,   10
Upon a sore injunction. My sweet mistress
Weeps when she sees me work, and says, such baseness
Had never like executor. I forget.
But these sweet thoughts do even refresh my labours,
Most busy lest, when I do it.

Enter MIRANDA; *and* PROSPERO *at a distance, unseen*

MIRANDA :   Alas, now pray you
Work not so hard. I would the lightning had
Burnt up those logs that you are enjoined to pile.
Pray, set it down and rest you. When this burns,
'T will weep for having wearied you. My father
Is hard at study; pray now rest yourself: 20
He 's safe for these three hours.
FERDINAND :   O most dear mistress,

III

23-4 *If . . . that.* What actions are appropriate?

26 *crack*, strain, tear.

28 *become*, be as proper for.

30 *to*, inclined to.

31 *worm*, creature. *infected*, i.e. with the disease of love.

32 *visitation*, (*a*) visit to comfort Ferdinand, (*b*) spread of the plague (Kermode).

34 *I . . . you.* Any gesture or movement?

35 *set it*, i.e., like a jewel.

37 *hest*, command.

37-8 *Admired . . . admiration.* Ferdinand plays on the meaning of Miranda, worthy of admiration, or wonder.

40 *best regard*, favourable glance.

41-2 *hath . . . ear*, has captivated my too readily attentive ear.

42 *several*, particular.

44 *full*, perfect, complete.

45 *owed*, possessed.

46 *put . . . foil*, (*a*) i.e. overthrew it, (*b*) showed up by contrast, (*c*) perhaps an echo after 'quarrel' of 'foil', a sword.

46-8 *O . . . best.* The platonic view of perfect beauty. See *As You Like It*, III. ii, 123-40.

48 *creature's*, created thing's.

The sun will set before I shall discharge
What I must strive to do.

MIRANDA: If you 'll sit down,
I 'll bear your logs the while. Pray give me that;
I 'll carry it to the pile.

FERDINAND: No, precious creature,
I had rather crack my sinews, break my back,
Than you should such dishonour undergo,
While I sit lazy by.

MIRANDA: It would become me
As well as it does you, and I should do it
With much more ease; for my good will is to it,   30
And yours it is against.

PROSPERO: Poor worm, thou art infected.
This visitation shows it.

MIRANDA: You look wearily.

FERDINAND: No, noble mistress, 'tis fresh morning with me
When you are by at night. I do beseech you—
Chiefly that I might set it in my prayers—
What is your name?

MIRANDA: Miranda—O my father,
I have broke your hest to say so.

FERDINAND: Admired Miranda,
Indeed the top of admiration, worth
What 's dearest to the world. Full many a lady
I have eyed with best regard, and many a time   40
The harmony of their tongues hath into bondage
Brought my too diligent ear. For several virtues
Have I liked several women, never any
With so full soul, but some defect in her
Did quarrel with the noblest grace she owed,
And put it to the foil. But you, O you,
So perfect and so peerless, are created
Of every creature's best.

51   *call men.* 'Hag seed' excluded.

52   *features*, appearances, i.e. of the whole person.

53   *skilless*, ignorant.

53–4   *modesty . . . dower.* Proverbial. Miranda stresses her sincerity.

57   *to like of*, that I should like.

59   *condition*, rightful position.

61   *I . . . so*, I wish it were not so, i.e. that his father was still alive.

63   *blow*, foul.

67   *Do . . . me?* Is Miranda—a go-getter, predatory female, frank, simple, sincere, naive?

68   *sound*, utterance.

69   *kind event*, happy ending.

70   *hollowly*, falsely.

70–1   *invert . . . mischief*, turn to disaster the best that fortune has in store for me.

75   *rare*, excellent, fine. *rain grace*. See IV. i, 18; V. i, 201–2.

76   *that . . . 'em*, the love that grows between them.

MIRANDA: I do not know
One of my sex; no woman's face remember,
Save, from my glass, mine one. Nor have I seen   50
More that I may call men than you good friend,
And my dear father. How features are abroad,
I am skilless of; but by my modesty,
The jewel in my dower, I would not wish
Any companion in the world but you.
Nor can imagination form a shape,
Besides yourself, to like of. But I prattle
Something too wildly, and my father's precepts
I therein do forget.

FERDINAND: I am, in my condition,
A prince, Miranda; I do think, a king—   60
I would, not so—and would no more endure
This wooden slavery than to suffer
The flesh-fly blow my mouth. Hear my soul speak.
The very instant that I saw you, did
My heart fly to your service; there resides,
To make me slave to it; and for your sake
Am I this patient log-man.

MIRANDA: Do you love me?

FERDINAND: O heaven, O earth, bear witness to this sound,
And crown what I profess with kind event
If I speak true. If hollowly, invert   70
What best is boded me to mischief. I
Beyond all limit of what else i' th' world
Do love, prize, honour you.

MIRANDA: I am a fool
To weep at what I am glad of.

PROSPERO: Fair encounter
Of two most rare affections. Heavens rain grace
On that which breeds between 'em.

FERDINAND: Wherefore weep you?

78   *take*, dare take.

80   *it*, my love. Miranda hesitates to use the word 'love'.

84   *maid*, (*a*) servant, (*b*) unmarried for your sake. *fellow*, equal, mate.

87   *thus humble*. More characteristics of romance and fairy tale where the lady as a page accompanies her lover. Should Ferdinand—kneel, kiss her hand or her dress, bow, embrace her?

89   *As . . . freedom*, as ever a slave is to be free. *here's my hand*, i.e. a hand-tokening betrothal.

91   *thousand thousand*, i.e. farewells.
      Do they depart simultaneously, does Ferdinand see her away, is there any lingering or gesture?

93   *Who . . . withal*, whom love has surprised with wonder.

94   *book*, i.e. for magical studies.

The Island

S.D.   Are the three drunk, sober, merry?

1   *Tell not me*, i.e. that the bottle is empty. *out*, empty.

2   *bear . . . 'em*, carry on and drink up. Literally, 'sail towards the enemy and board his ship'.

4   *folly*, freak (Kermode). Alternatively it is possible that Trinculo surprised at the title servant-monster, which he thinks is absurd, comments, 'The folly that overtakes people on this island'.

MIRANDA : At mine unworthiness, that dare not offer
  What I desire to give, and much less take
  What I shall die to want. But this is trifling,
  And all the more it seeks to hide itself,   80
  The bigger bulk it shows. Hence bashful cunning,
  And prompt me plain and holy innocence.
  I am your wife, if you will marry me;
  If not, I 'll die your maid. To be your fellow
  You may deny me, but I 'll be your servant
  Whether you will or no.
FERDINAND :   My mistress, dearest,
  And I thus humble ever.
MIRANDA :   My husband then?
FERDINAND : Ay, with a heart as willing
  As bondage e'er of freedom. Here 's my hand.
MIRANDA : And mine, with my heart in 't. And now farewell 90
  Till half an hour hence.
FERDINAND :   A thousand thousand.
                  [Exeunt Ferdinand and Miranda severally
PROSPERO : So glad of this as they I cannot be,
  Who are surprised withal; but my rejoicing
  At nothing can be more. I 'll to my book,
  For yet ere supper-time must I perform
  Much business appertaining.   *[Exit*

SCENE TWO

Enter CALIBAN, STEPHANO, *and* TRINCULO

STEPHANO : Tell not me; when the butt is out, we will drink
  water, not a drop before; therefore bear up, and board 'em.
  Servant-monster, drink to me.
TRINCULO : Servant-monster? The folly of this island. They say

7–8   *Thy . . . head*, i.e. staring and glazed with drink. See *Twelfth Night*, V. i, 204–5.

9   *set*, placed naturally.

11   *man-monster*, man = servant. *drowned . . . sack*, i.e. is speechless from drink.

14   *standard*, standard-bearer.

15   *standard*, one who stands upright. Caliban is too drunk to stand.

16   *run*, i.e. from the enemy.

17   *go*, walk. *lie*, (*a*) lie down, (*b*) tell lies.

23   *am . . . to*, feel man enough to.

24   *justle*, push, knock. *deboshed*, debauched, drink-sodden.

24–5   *was . . . sack*. Proverbially wine was the whetstone of valour.

26–7   *Wilt . . . monster*. 'Monstrous' can mean unnatural, deformed, gigantic, outrageous, or simply, of the nature of a monster. Trinculo argues that as Caliban is half-fish and half-monster he can tell only half-monstrous lies.

30   *natural*, (*a*) idiot, 'a natural', (*b*) as a monster is 'unnatural' it is paradoxical to call him 'natural'.

35–6   *I . . . thee*. Caliban is learning the arts of a courtier.

36   *suit*, request.

there's but five upon this isle; we are three of them; if th' other
two be brained like us, the state totters.

STEPHANO: Drink servant-monster when I bid thee. Thy eyes
are almost set in thy head.

TRINCULO: Where should they be set else? He were a brave
monster indeed if they were set in his tail.   10

STEPHANO: My man-monster hath drowned his tongue in sack.
For my part the sea cannot drown me; I swam, ere I could recover the shore, five and thirty leagues off and on. By this light
thou shalt be my lieutenant, monster, or my standard.

TRINCULO: Your lieutenant if you list, he's no standard.

STEPHANO: We'll not run Monsieur Monster.

TRINCULO: Nor go neither. But you'll lie like dogs, and yet
say nothing neither.

STEPHANO: Moon-calf, speak once in thy life, if thou beest a
good moon-calf.   20

CALIBAN: How does thy honour? Let me lick thy shoe.
I'll not serve him, he is not valiant.

TRINCULO: Thou liest most ignorant monster, I am in case to
justle a constable. Why, thou deboshed fish thou, was there
ever man a coward that hath drunk so much sack as I today?
Wilt thou tell a monstrous lie, being but half a fish, and half
a monster?

CALIBAN: Lo, how he mocks me. Wilt thou let him my lord?

TRINCULO: 'Lord' quoth he? That a monster should be such
a natural.   30

CALIBAN: Lo, lo, again. Bite him to death I prithee.

STEPHANO: Trinculo, keep a good tongue in your head. If you
prove a mutineer—the next tree. The poor monster's my
subject, and he shall not suffer indignity.

CALIBAN: I thank my noble lord. Wilt thou be pleased to
hearken once again to the suit I made to thee?

STEPHANO: Marry will I. Kneel and repeat it. I will stand, and
so shall Trinculo.

S.D.   Where does Ariel place himself in relation to the others?

42   *jesting monkey*. A glance at Trinculo, the jester. *monkey*, i.e. meddlesome interferer.

46   *supplant*, knock out, uproot.

48   *Mum*, silence.

52   *this thing*, Trinculo.

55   *compassed*, brought about.

56   *party*, person.

57–8   *I'll . . . head*. An echo of *Judges*, iv. 21. Why? Caliban is actuated solely by the desire for revenge even though it will subordinate him to another master.

60   *pied ninny*, (*a*) a glance at Trinculo's motley, (*b*) Hilda Hulme suggests an allusion to Trinculo's mischievous chattering, and cites chatterpie, magpie. *scurvy patch*, (*a*) wretched jester or idiot, (*b*) scab.

64   *quick freshes*, fresh springs.

67   *make . . . thee*, beat you as dried cod is beaten before it is boiled.

Act Three, Scene Two

Enter ARIEL, *invisible*

CALIBAN: As I told thee before, I am subject to a tyrant, a
sorcerer, that by his cunning hath cheated me of the island.

ARIEL: Thou liest.   41

CALIBAN: Thou liest, thou jesting monkey thou.
I would my valiant master would destroy thee!
I do not lie.

STEPHANO: Trinculo, if you trouble him any more in 's tale, by
this hand, I will supplant some of your teeth.

TRINCULO: Why, I said nothing.

STEPHANO: Mum then, and no more. Proceed.

CALIBAN: I say, by sorcery he got this isle;
From me he got it. If thy greatness will,   50
Revenge it on him, for I know thou darest,
But this thing dare not.

STEPHANO: That 's most certain.

CALIBAN: Thou shalt be lord of it, and I 'll serve thee.

STEPHANO: How now shall this be compassed? Canst thou bring
me to the party?

CALIBAN: Yea, yea my lord, I 'll yield him thee asleep,
Where thou mayst knock a nail into his head.

ARIEL: Thou liest, thou canst not.

CALIBAN: What a pied ninny's this. Thou scurvy patch!   60
I do beseech thy greatness, give him blows,
And take his bottle from him. When that 's gone,
He shall drink nought but brine, for I'll not show him
Where the quick freshes are.

STEPHANO: Trinculo, run into no further danger. Interrupt the
monster one word further, and by this hand, I 'll turn my mercy
out o' doors, and make a stock-fish of thee.

TRINCULO: Why, what did I? I did nothing. I 'll go farther off.

STEPHANO: Didst thou not say he lied?

ARIEL: Thou liest.   70

STEPHANO: Do I so? Take thou that.   [*Beats Trinculo*]

73–4   *and hearing too*, you cannot hear properly either.

75   *murrain*, cattle disease.

77–8   *Prithee . . . off.* Is this addressed to Trinculo so that there is no further interruption, or to Caliban? (See II. ii, 24–5.) Any threatening gesture?

83   *Having . . . books*, i.e. to deprive Prospero of his magical powers.
84   *paunch*, stab him in the belly.
85   *wezand*, wind-pipe.

87   *sot*, weak fool.
88–9   *They . . . I.* Any other evidence of this? It was a common belief that spirits were rebellious to human command.
89   *Burn . . . books*, (*a*) only be sure to burn his books, (*b*) burn nothing but his books. The latter might explain the mention of 'brave utensils' which 'must not be burnt' (Kermode).
90   *utensils.* Pronounced útensils. Does Caliban hesitate over this word and over 'nonpareil' (l. 94)?
94   *nonpareil*, unmatchable in beauty.

101   *save our graces!* Any gestures?

As you like this, give me the lie another time.

TRINCULO: I did not give the lie. Out o' your wits and hearing too? A pox o' your bottle, this can sack and drinking do. A murrain on your monster, and the devil take your fingers!

CALIBAN: Ha, ha, ha!

STEPHANO: Now, forward with your tale. Prithee stand farther off.

CALIBAN: Beat him enough. After a little time
I'll beat him too.

STEPHANO: Stand farther. Come proceed.   80

CALIBAN: Why, as I told thee, 't is a custom with him
I' th' afternoon to sleep. There thou mayst brain him,
Having first seized his books, or with a log
Batter his skull, or paunch him with a stake,
Or cut his wezand with thy knife. Remember
First to possess his books; for without them
He 's but a sot, as I am, nor hath not
One spirit to command. They all do hate him
As rootedly as I. Burn but his books.
He has brave utensils—for so he calls them—   90
Which, when he has a house, he 'll deck withal.
And that most deeply to consider is
The beauty of his daughter. He himself
Calls her a nonpareil. I never saw a woman,
But only Sycorax my dam and she;
But she as far surpasseth Sycorax
As great'st does least.

STEPHANO: Is it so brave a lass?

CALIBAN: Ay lord. She will become thy bed, I warrant,
And bring thee forth brave brood.   99

STEPHANO: Monster, I will kill this man. His daughter and I will be king and queen—save our graces!—and Trinculo and thyself shall be viceroys. Dost thou like the plot, Trinculo?

TRINCULO: Excellent.

107   *Ay . . . honour*. Hardly an apt oath for Stephano.

110   *troll*, roll out, roar out. *catch*, a song for three or more voices. When the first singer reached the end of the first line, the second singer began the first line, and so on.

112   *do reason*, do anything reasonable.

        They arrange themselves. Should one of them conduct the other two?

114   *Flout*, mock. *scout*, taunt. Dover Wilson and Kermode keep the Folio reading 'cout', i.e. 'colt', cheat or fool, although this word is not otherwise recorded until the nineteenth century.

116   *Thought is free*. Proverbial.

117   *That's . . . tune*. Presumably the discordant noise has caused them to stop.

S.D.   *tabor*, side drum.

119–   *picture of Nobody*. A woodcut of Nobody, a man with head, legs
20   and arms but no body, appeared on numerous broadsheets in the seventeenth century.

122   *take 't . . . list*, take what shape you please.

124   *He . . . debts*. A proverb to console himself. The point of the proverb was stressed by the pun, 'deaths' (pronounced 'dets') and 'debts'. See *1 Henry IV*, I. iii, 185–6.

124–5 *Mercy upon us!* Any action by Ariel to cause this sudden terror?

127   *No . . . I*. How does Stephano's behaviour give the lie to his words?

128   *noises*, music.

130   *twangling*, the sounding of stringed instruments.

131   *hum*, murmur.

131–3 *voices . . . again*, singing so sweet that it would lull me to sleep again.

        Does Caliban's speech reveal—the power of music over him, the frustration of dreams, some appreciation of beauty?

        Some see in Caliban's speech a reflection of a main theme of the

STEPHANO: Give me thy hand, I am sorry I beat thee. But while thou livest, keep a good tongue in thy head.

CALIBAN: Within this half hour will he be asleep.
Wilt thou destroy him then?

STEPHANO: Ay on mine honour.

ARIEL: This will I tell my master.

CALIBAN: Thou mak'st me merry. I am full of pleasure;
Let us be jocund. Will you troll the catch   110
You taught me but while-ere?

STEPHANO: At thy request monster, I will do reason, any reason.
Come on, Trinculo, let us sing.   [*Sings*

            Flout 'em and scout 'em
            And scout 'em and flout 'em;
                  Thought is free.

CALIBAN: That 's not the tune.
                    [*Ariel plays the tune on a tabor and pipe*

STEPHANO: What is this same?

TRINCULO: This is the tune of our catch, played by the picture of Nobody.   120

STEPHANO: If thou beest a man, show thyself in thy likeness; if thou beest a devil, take 't as thou list.

TRINCULO: O forgive me my sins.

STEPHANO: He that dies pays all debts. I defy thee. Mercy upon us!

CALIBAN: Art thou afeard?

STEPHANO: No monster, not I.

CALIBAN: Be not afeard, the isle is full of noises,
Sounds and sweet airs, that give delight and hurt not.
Sometimes a thousand twangling instruments   130
Will hum about mine ears; and sometime voices,
That if I then had waked after long sleep,
Will make me sleep again; and then in dreaming,
The clouds methought would open, and show riches
Ready to drop upon me, that when I waked,

play, the transformation of storm to calm, of disorder to harmony, of the transmutation of ugliness to strange beauty.

139   *When . . . destroyed.* Caliban is not put off their main task as are the others who are drawn away by the compulsive attraction of the music.

144   *he . . . on.* The drumming becomes more urgent.

145   *Wilt come?* Probably spoken to Caliban who is reluctant to follow the music. Do they depart reeling, dancing, capering, fearfully, stealthily, trance-like (see IV. i, 171–84)?

       Ironically Stephano and Trinculo are under Caliban's leadership, the demi-devil is instructing the drunkards to become beasts.

The Island

S.D.   Their entry should show their weariness. Perhaps Alonso and Gonzalo should be assisted. On what do they sit (ll. 4, 6)?

1   *lakin*, little lady, Virgin Mary.

2–3   *a . . . meanders.* The formal mazes in gardens were sometimes constructed of straight paths (forthrights) and winding or circular paths (meanders).

5   *attached*, seized, arrested.

6   *To*, which results in. *spirits*, faculties.

8   *for my flatterer*, to flatter me.

10   *frustrate*, vain. Alonso's grief is a necessary prelude to repentance.

12   *for one repulse*, because of one setback.

13   *advantage*, opportunity.

14   *throughly*, thoroughly.

I cried to dream again.

STEPHANO: This will prove a brave kingdom to me, where I shall have my music for nothing.

CALIBAN: When Prospero is destroyed.

STEPHANO: That shall be by and by. I remember the story.   140

TRINCULO: The sound is going away. Let's follow it, and after do our work.

STEPHANO: Lead monster, we'll follow. I would I could see this taborer, he lays it on.

TRINCULO: Wilt come? I'll follow, Stephano.   [*Exeunt*

SCENE THREE

Enter ALONSO, SEBASTIAN, ANTONIO, GONZALO,
ADRIAN, FRANCISCO, *etc.*

GONZALO: By 'r lakin, I can go no farther, sir;
My old bones ache. Here's a maze trod indeed
Through forthrights and meanders. By your patience,
I needs must rest me.

ALONSO: Old lord, I cannot blame thee,
Who am myself attached with weariness
To the dulling of my spirits. Sit down, and rest.
Even here I will put off my hope, and keep it
No longer for my flatterer. He is drowned
Whom thus we stray to find, and the sea mocks
Our frustrate search on land. Well, let him go.   10

ANTONIO: [*Aside to Sebastian*] I am right glad that he's so out of hope.
Do not, for one repulse, forego the purpose
That you resolved t' effect.

SEBASTIAN: [*Aside to Antonio*] The next advantage
Will we take throughly.

s.D.   *on the top.* According to Adams Prospero was in the musicians'
       room and not on the balcony at the back of the stage. He adds
       that Prospero's presence is not dramatically necessary but that here
       he is coordinating the music with the spectacle. Adams, however,
       overlooks the fact that Prospero except for the first scene is always
       present during the main displays of his magic. Not only is this
       dramatically telling but it keeps the audience aware that the spirits
       are under control and are not diabolic. *strange Shapes.* Perhaps
       creatures from mythology or from the medieval bestiaries. *dance.*
       In a manuscript in the British Museum, Add. 10444, there is a
       dance entitled 'The Tempest'. It has been suggested by Cutts that
       it was composed by Robert Johnson and that it belongs here.
       Perhaps a pavane is the type of dance required. The banquet and
       harpy spectacles are vivid representations of the direction of the
       play. The tantalean banquet was not uncommon (see *Timon of
       Athens*, III. vi), and was intended to be interpreted allegorically.
       Solemn . . . music. Probably recorders.

18–19 *What . . . music.* Music indicating the presence of the super-
       natural as well as accompanying the dance.

20   *kind keepers,* guardian angels.

21   *living drollery,* a fantastic, grotesque picture—not a puppet show
       (Shaaber).

22   *unicorns.* The unicorn was a legendary animal with a horse's body
       and a horn protruding from its forehead.

23   *one tree.* Much debated—perhaps the cedar. *phœnix.* A mythical
       bird with gorgeous plumage, fabled to be the only one of its
       kind, and to live for five hundred years, after which it burnt
       itself to ashes on a pyre and sprang from the ashes with renewed
       youth. The two creatures were noted for their rarity and as
       symbols of chastity.

26   *Travellers . . . lie.* Proverbially travellers did lie.

31   *monstrous shape,* i.e. of imaginary creatures.

33   *generation,* kind, race.

36   *muse,* wonder at.

ANTONIO: [*Aside to Sebastian*] Let it be tonight;
For, now they are oppressed with travel, they
Will not, nor cannot, use such vigilance
As when they are fresh.

Enter PROSPERO *on the top, invisible. Enter several strange Shapes,*
bringing in a banquet; they dance about it with gentle actions of
salutation; and, inviting the King, &c., to eat, they depart
[*Solemn and strange* music

SEBASTIAN: [*Aside to Antonio*] I say, tonight. No more.
ALONSO: What harmony is this? My good friends, hark.
GONZALO: Marvellous sweet music.
ALONSO: Give us kind keepers, heavens. What were these?
SEBASTIAN: A living drollery. Now I will believe   21
That there are unicorns; that in Arabia
There is one tree, the phœnix' throne, one phœnix
At this hour reigning there.
ANTONIO: I 'll believe both.
And what does else want credit, come to me,
And I 'll be sworn 't is true. Travellers ne'er did lie.
Though fools at home condemn 'em.
GONZALO: If in Naples
I should report this now, would they believe me?
If I should say, I saw such islanders—
For certes these are people of the island—   30
Who though they are of monstrous shape, yet note,
Their manners are more gentle-kind than of
Our human generation you shall find
Many, nay almost any.
PROSPERO: [*Aside*] Honest lord,
Thou hast said well. For some of you there present
Are worse than devils.
ALONSO: I cannot too much muse
Such shapes, such gesture, and such sound expressing—

39   *excellent dumb discourse*, eloquent miming. *Praise in departing*. Proverbially you keep your praise for your host until you know how his hospitality will end.

45   *Dew-lapped*, with loose flesh hanging from their throats, goitre.

46   *Wallets*, bags especially for carrying on the back. See Appendix I.

46-7   *men . . . breasts*. Also mentioned in *Othello*, I. iii, 144-5, described in Ralegh's *Discovery of Guiana* and Hackluyt, *Principal Navigations*.

48   *Each . . . one*. Travellers about to journey abroad frequently deposited a sum of money with an underwriter under contract that they would receive five times the amount of the deposit when they returned. If they failed to return, the underwriter retained the deposit.

49   *Good warrant*, clear proof.

      Does Ariel enter—by a trap door, by wire from the 'heavens', through the normal entry door?

S.D.   *harpy*. The harpies were identified with the furies of classical myth, who carry out divine vengeance on mortals. In the *Æneid* the harpies seize the banquet the Trojans are about to eat, and Celæno, the eldest of the furies prophesies the punishment of hunger that will befall them. The Trojans seek for pardon with vows and promised offerings for trying to drive the harpies away. They are beautiful virginal creatures of the wind, air, and storm and accordingly are winged and taloned like eagles. So Ariel, the beautiful spirit of the air, who made the storm of the first scene, is also a Harpy-Fury who troubles the minds of the three sinners (D. C. Allen, *Image and Meaning*, pp. 42–66). Ariel's dress should be spectacular with brilliantly coloured wings and feathers and ostentatious claws. *claps his wings*. A cover for the disappearance of the banquet perhaps into the table.

53   *three . . . sin*, Alonso, Antonio, and Sebastian.

54   *to instrument*, as the means of accomplishing its purposes.

55   *never-surfeited*, ever hungry, never satisfied.

56   *belch up*, i.e. you are so wicked that even the sea contrary to its nature has vomited you forth.

56-8   *and . . . live*, i.e. and further, being unfit to live with your fellow men you are thrown on this island where no men live.

58   *I . . . mad*. What actions are appropriate?

59   *such-like valour*, frantic recklessness.

60   *proper*, own, i.e. themselves.

Although they want the use of tongue—a kind
Of excellent dumb discourse.

PROSPERO: [*Aside*] Praise in departing.

FRANCISCO: They vanished strangely.

SEBASTIAN: No matter, since   40
They have left their viands behind; for we have stomachs.
Will 't please you taste of what is here?

ALONSO: Not I.

GONZALO: Faith sir, you need not fear. When we were boys,
Who would believe that there were mountaineers
Dew-lapped like bulls, whose throats had hanging at 'em
Wallets of flesh? Or that there were such men
Whose heads stood in their breasts? Which now we find
Each putter-out of five for one will bring us
Good warrant of.

ALONSO: I will stand to, and feed,
Although my last: no matter, since I feel   50
The best is past. Brother, my lord the Duke,
Stand to, and do as we.

Thunder and lightning. Enter ARIEL, *like a harpy; claps his wings
upon the table; and, with a quaint device, the banquet vanishes*

ARIEL: You are three men of sin, whom Destiny,
That hath to instrument this lower world
And what is in 't, the never-surfeited sea
Hath caused to belch up you, and on this island
Where man doth not inhabit, you 'mongst men
Being most unfit to live. I have made you mad;
And even with such-like valour men hang, and drown
Their proper selves.   [*They draw swords*

60–5   *I . . . plume*, either (*a*) I and my fellows are the elements (? fire, air) of which your swords are tempered and therefore they cannot wound us, or (*b*) I and my fellows are ministers of Destiny and therefore the elements, which are ruled by Destiny and of which your swords are made, can have no power over us.

63   *bemocked-at*, ridiculous.

64   *still-closing*, ever closing up.

65   *dowle*, feather, piece of fluff. *plume*. Ariel is wearing a feathered headdress, perhaps a crest of feathers. *fellow-ministers*. Perhaps other spirits as harpies attend on Ariel.

66   *If*, even if.

67–8   *Your . . . uplifted*. What visual evidence of this—any magical gesture by Ariel, any attempt to lift their swords?

71   *requit it*, paid you back for your crime.

74   *creatures*, created things.

75   *peace*, (*a*) security, (*b*) peace of mind.

77   *perdition*, destruction.

78   *Can . . . once*, i.e. sudden.

79   *whose*, i.e. powers (l. 73).

81–2   *is . . . ensuing*, is only grief, repentance, and a blameless life in the future.

s.d.   Ariel's departure should be consistent with his entry, l. 53.
       mocks and mows, grimaces, silent gestures of mockery and jeering.
       What is Alonso's party doing now and during Prospero's following speech—cowering, rigid in a tableaux, paralysed with fear?

83–6   *Bravely . . . say*. Has Ariel joined Prospero 'on the top'?

83   *Bravely*, splendidly.

84   *a . . . devouring*, a ravishing grace (Kermode points out that 'devouring' is specially appropriate to a harpy).

85   *bated*, omitted.

87   *observation strange*, rare carrying out of instructions, wonderful observance of orders.

You fools, I and my fellows   60
Are ministers of Fate: the elements,
Of whom your swords are tempered, may as well
Wound the loud winds, or with bemocked-at stabs
Kill the still-closing waters, as diminish
One dowle that 's in my plume. My fellow-ministers
Are like invulnerable. If you could hurt,
Your swords are now too massy for your strengths,
And will not be uplifted. But remember—
For that 's my business to you—that you three
From Milan did supplant good Prospero;   70
Exposed unto the sea, which hath requit it,
Him and his innocent child. For which foul deed
The powers, delaying, not forgetting, have
Incensed the seas and shores, yea, all the creatures,
Against your peace. Thee of thy son, Alonso,
They have bereft; and do pronounce by me
Lingering perdition—worse than any death
Can be at once—shall step by step attend
You, and your ways; whose wraths to guard you from—
Which here, in this most desolate isle, else falls   80
Upon your heads—is nothing but heart's sorrow
And a clear life ensuing.

He vanishes in thunder; then, to soft music, enter the Shapes again,
and dance, with mocks and mows, and carrying out the table

PROSPERO: Bravely the figure of this harpy hast thou
    Performed, my Ariel; a grace it had, devouring.
    Of my instruction hast thou nothing bated
    In what thou hadst to say. So with good life
    And observation strange, my meaner ministers

133

88   *several kinds*, separate duties according to their natures. *high*, mighty.

89–90 *knit . . . distractions*, entangled in their own disordered minds. The hinted paradox in 'knit' and 'distracted' stresses their confusion.

91   *fits*, desperate states.

91–2 *while . . . Ferdinand*. Prospero usually announces his intentions when about to leave the stage. What dramatic value has this?

95   *monstrous*, horrible, i.e. his crime.

96–9 *Methought . . . trespass*. All nature, the instrument of destiny, is reminding Alonso of his guilt. Any action or gesture?

99   *bass*, utter in a deep tone. The jingle with 'trespass' is emphatic.

101   *plummet*, lead-line, sounding-lead.
      Is Alonso—despairing, hysterical, terrified, frenzied?

102–3 *But . . . second*. Sebastian and Antonio see only evil in the spectacle. Why? It rouses desperate courage in them.

104–6 *All . . . spirits*. Did Gonzalo hear Ariel's words?

108   *ecstasy*, frenzy, madness.
      Is this scene purgatorial, the infliction of punishment by the frustration of desire, the temporary breaking down of reason, or the sudden illumination of truth and guilt by vision or spectacle?

Their several kinds have done. My high charms work,
And these mine enemies are all knit up
In their distractions. They now are in my power,   90
And in these fits I leave them, while I visit
Young Ferdinand, whom they suppose is drowned,
And his, and mine loved darling.   [*Exit*

GONZALO: I' the name of something holy, sir, why stand you
   In this strange stare?

ALONSO: O, it is monstrous, monstrous.
   Methought the billows spoke, and told me of it;
   The winds did sing it to me; and the thunder,
   That deep and dreadful organ-pipe, pronounced
   The name of Prosper. It did bass my trespass.
   Therefore my son i' th' ooze is bedded; and   100
   I 'll seek him deeper than e'er plummet sounded,
   And with him there lie mudded.   [*Exit*

SEBASTIAN: But one fiend at a time,
   I 'll fight their legions o'er.

ANTONIO: I 'll be thy second.
                           [*Exeunt Sebastian and Antonio*

GONZALO: All three of them are desperate. Their great guilt,
   Like poison given to work a great time after,
   Now 'gins to bite the spirits. I do beseech you,
   That are of suppler joints, follow them swiftly,
   And hinder them from what this ecstasy
   May now provoke them to.

ADRIAN: Follow, I pray you.   [*Exeunt*

S.D.   Should Prospero lead Miranda in, or should Miranda and Ferdinand be together?

1   *punished*, i.e. to test his love but on the pretence that he was a spy (I. ii, 459–63).

3   *third*. Some editors prefer 'thread', or 'thrid' which is a variant spelling of both thread and third. 'Third', however, can be satisfactorily interpreted in various ways. See also V. i, 311.

4–5   *who . . . hand*. Any accompanying action?

7   *strangely*, wonderfully.

7–8   *Here . . . gift*. What action would be suitable—joining their hands, raising one hand heavenwards, holding their hands in his?

9   *her off*. Dover Wilson prefers 'hereof'.

11   *halt*, limp.

12   *Against an oracle*, even though an oracle pronounced it otherwise.

13–14   *acquisition . . . purchased*. Shakespeare, regarding love as a kind of wealth, frequently uses the imagery of commerce and merchandise to describe its winning, *Romeo and Juliet*, III. ii, 26–8, 82–4; *Love's Labour's Lost*, V. ii, 198–200.

16   *sanctimonious*, holy, sacred.

18–19   *sweet . . . grow*. i.e. the heavens will not bless this marriage with children. For a similar dew or rain imagery see III. i, 75–6 and *Henry VIII*, IV. ii, 133. Kermode notes the 'strongly religious overtone (cf. the *asperges* of the Mass)'. See also *A Midsummer Night's Dream*, V. i, 389–406.

19   *barren*. In contrast with the fertility theme of the previous sentence.

20   *sour-eyed*. In contrast with 'sweet'.

21   *weeds so loathly*. See *Richard II*, III. iv, 38–9,
        The noisome weeds which without profit suck
        The soil's fertility.

22–3   *Therefore . . . you*, therefore take care to act only in accordance with strict marriage vows, or, following Kittredge, 'take care, and so Hymen's lamps will burn with a clear, favourable flame for you.'

23   *Hymen*. The Roman god of marriage, represented as a young man wearing a yellow robe and carrying a torch.

136

ACT FOUR

SCENE ONE

Enter PROSPERO, FERDINAND, *and* MIRANDA

PROSPERO : If I have too austerely punished you,
    Your compensation makes amends, for I
    Have given you here a third of mine own life,
    Or that for which I live; who once again
    I tender to thy hand. All thy vexations
    Were but my trials of thy love, and thou
    Hast strangely stood the test. Here, afore Heaven
    I ratify this my rich gift. O Ferdinand,
    Do not smile at me that I boast her off,
    For thou shalt find she will outstrip all praise,   10
    And make it halt behind her.
FERDINAND :   I do believe it
    Against an oracle.
PROSPERO : Then, as my gift, and thine own acquisition
    Worthily purchased, take my daughter. But
    If thou dost break her virgin-knot before
    All sanctimonious ceremonies may
    With full and holy rite be ministered,
    No sweet aspersion shall the heavens let fall
    To make this contract grow; but barren hate,
    Sour-eyed disdain, and discord shall bestrew   20
    The union of your bed with weeds so loathly
    That you shall hate it both. Therefore take heed.
    As Hymen's lamps shall light you.
FERDINAND :   As I hope

24   *fair issue*, perfectly formed children.

26   *suggestion*, temptation.

27   *worser genius*. Each human being was supposed to have a good and a bad angel or spirit which struggled for the possession of his soul. *genius*, spirit. *can*, can make. *melt*, i.e. with the heat of desire.

29   *edge*, keen enjoyment (Kermode).

30–1 *or . . . below*, either the horses of the sun-god's chariot have gone lame, or night has been imprisoned in the underworld and does not appear, i.e. daylight lingers far too long or night delays its coming.

30   *Phœbus*. In classical myth the sun god.

32   *Sit . . . own*. The two sit apart in readiness for viewing the masque.

33   *What*, come.

S.D. *Enter Ariel*. Is he invisible to Ferdinand and Miranda? How does he enter—by air, normally, by trap door?

37   *trick*, elaborate device of pageantry. *rabble*, i.e. meaner spirits.

41   *vanity*, show, trifle.

42   *Presently?* at once?

43   *twink*, twinkling of an eye.

47   *mop and mow*, grins and smiles.

48   *Do . . . no?* Is Ariel joyous, pouting, affectionate, effervescent?

50   *Well, I conceive*, very good, I understand.

51–4 *Look . . . vow*. What causes this iteration—Prospero's anxiety arising from his own suspicious temperament, the enthusiastic embracements of the two while he has been talking to Ariel, and the absence of a chaperon to advise Miranda, her ignorance of the

For quiet days, fair issue, and long life,
With such love as 'tis now, the murkiest den,
The most opportune place, the strong'st suggestion
Our worser genius can, shall never melt
Mine honour into lust, to take away
The edge of that day's celebration,
When I shall think or Phœbus' steeds are foundered,   30
Or Night kept chained below.
PROSPERO: Fairly spoke.
Sit then, and talk with her, she is thine own.
What Ariel, my industrious servant Ariel!

Enter ARIEL

ARIEL: What would my potent master? Here I am.
PROSPERO: Thou, and thy meaner fellows, your last service
Did worthily perform. And I must use you
In such another trick. Go bring the rabble,
O'er whom I give thee power, here to this place.
Incite them to quick motion, for I must
Bestow upon the eyes of this young couple   40
Some vanity of mine art. It is my promise,
And they expect it from me.
ARIEL: Presently?
PROSPERO: Ay, with a twink.
ARIEL: Before you can say, 'come', and 'go',
                And breathe twice, and cry, 'so, so',
                Each one tripping on his toe,
                Will be here with mop and mow.
                Do you love me master? No?
PROSPERO: Dearly, my delicate Ariel. Do not approach
Till thou dost hear me call.
ARIEL: Well, I conceive.   [*Exit*   50
PROSPERO: Look thou be true. Do not give dalliance

world, that chastity is Miranda's only dowry, that absolute purity is essential in anything concerned with Prospero's magic?

51 *dalliance*, love-making.

52 *Too . . . rein*, too much freedom. *oaths*. A quibble on 'oats'. Compare the pun on 'goats' and 'Goths' (*As You Like It*, III. iii, 5–6) and see *Henry V*, II. iii, 51. *straw*, i.e. easily burnt.

55–6 *The . . . liver*, the pure, chaste thoughts that Miranda inspires in my heart cool my desires.

56 *liver*. Believed to be the organ responsible for the physical aspects of love.

57 *corollary*, abundance, over-many.

58 *pertly*, nimbly, briskly.

59 *No . . . silent*. Silence was essential if magic was to work successfully.

S.D. *Soft music*. What instruments—recorders, lutes, oboes, viols? *Iris*. In classical myth the goddess of the rainbow and divine messenger. Her introduction here forms an apt structural link with the previous scene since she was sister of the harpies. Northrop Frye (Pelican edition) in view of the fertility theme of the masque makes the further point that the rainbow after the tempest of the Flood was the sign of God's promise to mankind that 'seedtime and harvest . . . shall not cease' *Genesis*, viii. 22; ix. 12–13. Nicoll cites for her costume a 'robe of discoloured taffeta, figured in variable colours like the rainbow, a cloudy wreath on her head', and saffron coloured wings.

63 *stover*, cloves and coarse grass dried for winter cattle food.

64 *pioned . . . brims*. Editors consider that this describes (*a*) flowers on river banks, (*b*) river banks trenched and supported by interwoven branches, or (*c*) field boundaries of earth banks with layered hedges on top. It is doubtful what flowers were intended, orchids and marsh marigolds have been suggested. The latter gains some support from the 'cup-like twill-plants' of Chapman's *Ovid's Banquet of Sense*.

65 *hest*, command.

66 *broom-groves*. Perhaps a reminiscence of Virgil's *Georgics*, II, 434: 'The willow and the humble broom—why they either supply leaves to the herd, or shade to the shepherd' (W. P. Mustard). The broom gives little shade. A cypress-like tree may be intended.

68 *lass-lorn*, jilted, forsaken. *poll-clipt*, pruned, pollarded. Vines were cut back in February.

70 *air*, refresh yourself. *queen . . . sky*, Juno, wife of Jupiter.

S.D. *Juno descends*. This may be a prompter's advance notice. On the

Too much the rein. The strongest oaths are straw
To the fire i' th' blood. Be more abstemious,
Or else good night your vow.
FERDINAND: I warrant you, sir,
The white cold virgin snow upon my heart
Abates the ardour of my liver.
PROSPERO: Well.
Now come my Ariel, bring a corollary,
Rather than want a spirit. Appear, and pertly.
No tongue. All eyes. Be silent.   [*Soft music*

Enter IRIS

IRIS: Ceres, most bounteous lady, thy rich leas   60
Of wheat, rye, barley, vetches, oats, and pease;
Thy turfy mountains, where live nibbling sheep,
And flat meads thatched with stover, them to keep;
Thy banks with pioned and twilled brims,
Which spongy April at thy hest betrims,
To make cold nymphs chaste crowns; and thy broom-groves,
Whose shadow the dismissed bachelor loves,
Being lass-lorn; thy poll-clipt vineyard;
And thy sea-marge, sterile and rocky-hard,
Where thou thyself dost air;—the queen o' th' sky,   70
Whose watery arch and messenger am I,
Bids thee leave these, and with her sovereign grace,
                                        [*Juno descends*

other hand 'her peacocks fly amain' suggests that her chariot is in
view either alighting on the raised back-stage or descending from
the stage heavens.

74   *peacocks.* Sacred to Juno. They drew her chariot. *amain,* swiftly.

75   *Ceres.* Nicoll suggests her robe was straw-coloured, embroidered
with silver and adorned with ears of corn.

81   *bosky,* bushy.

82   *proud,* (*a*) to be so adorned, (*b*) teeming.

83   *short-grassed green.* Law suggests that this refers to the green baize
floor covering of the inner stage at Court.

85   *estate,* bestow. It has been suggested that at this point during the
performance at the royal wedding Juno and Ceres, according to
custom in court masques, presented a gift to Princess Elizabeth.

89   *dusky . . . got.* Dis, the god of the underworld, carried off Ceres'
daughter, Proserpine, while she was gathering flowers on the
slopes of Etna. She became his queen spending half the year with
him and half on earth.

90   *blind boy's,* Cupid's. *scandalled,* disgraceful, ill-reputed.

93   *Paphos.* A town in Cyprus, the centre of the worship of Venus.

94   *Dove-drawn.* Doves and sparrows were sacred to Venus.

95   *wanton,* unchaste.

96   *bed-right,* marriage privilege.

98   *Mars's hot minion,* the lustful darling of Mars. Mars and Venus were
lovers.

99   *waspish-headed son,* i.e. as quick to shoot an arrow as a wasp is to
sting. *has . . . arrows.* Cupid with broken arrows was part of the
emblem picture of chastity.

101   *of state,* stately.

Here on this grass-plot, in this very place,
To come and sport. Her peacocks fly amain.
Approach, rich Ceres, her to entertain.

Enter CERES

CERES: Hail, many-coloured messenger, that ne'er
 Dost disobey the wife of Jupiter;
 Who with thy saffron wings upon my flowers
 Diffusest honey-drops, refreshing showers,
 And with each end of thy blue bow dost crown   80
 My bosky acres and my unshrubbed down,
 Rich scarf to my proud earth. Why hath thy queen
 Summoned me hither, to this short-grassed green?
IRIS: A contract of true love to celebrate,
 And some donation freely to estate
 On the blest lovers.
CERES: Tell me heavenly bow,
 If Venus or her son, as thou dost know,
 Do now attend the queen? Since they did plot
 The means that dusky Dis my daughter got,
 Her and her blind boy's scandalled company   90
 I have forsworn.
IRIS: Of her society
 Be not afraid. I met her deity
 Cutting the clouds towards Paphos, and her son
 Dove-drawn with her. Here thought they to have done
 Some wanton charm upon this man and maid,
 Whose vows are, that no bed-right shall be paid
 Till Hymen's torch be lighted. But in vain;
 Mars's hot minion is returned again;
 Her waspish-headed son has broke his arrows,
 Swears he will shoot no more, but play with sparrows, 100
 And be a boy right out.
CERES: Highest queen of state,

102   *I . . . gait.* Juno's stately gait was a well-known attribute.

        Juno's costume in an earlier masque was a sky-coloured mantle embroidered with gold and figured with peacock's feathers. In another her attire was rich and like a queen, a white diadem on her head from whence descended a veil, and that bound with a fascia of several coloured silks set with all sorts of jewels and raised in the top with lilies and roses. In her right hand she held a sceptre, and in the other a timbrel.

103–5 *Go . . . issue.* Juno as the protector of marriage presided over weddings.

105   *issue*, children.

110   *foison*, abundance.

114–5 *Spring . . . harvest.* As Kermode and others note this is a wish for the Golden Age when there was no winter season and spring followed harvest. Dover Wilson sees in this evidence that the masque was inserted for the wedding of Princess Elizabeth and the Elector Palatine.

123   *So . . . father*, so excellent a father who performs wonders.

128   *Naiads*, water-nymphs. In another masque the water-nymphs wore sea-green taffeta, with bubbles of crystal intermixed with powdering of silver resembling drops of water, bluish tresses, and on their heads garlands of water lilies. Here they may have worn wreaths of sedges. *windring*. Perhaps a combination of 'wandering' and 'winding'.

Great Juno comes, I know her by her gait.

Enter JUNO

JUNO : How does my bounteous sister? Go with me
    To bless this twain, that they may prosperous be
    And honoured in their issue.   *[They sing*

JUNO :   Honour, riches, marriage-blessing,
            Long continuance, and increasing,
            Hourly joys be still upon you.
            Juno sings her blessings on you.

CERES :   Earth's increase, foison plenty,   110
            Barns and garners never empty,
            Vines with clustering bunches growing,
            Plants with goodly burthen bowing.

            Spring come to you at the farthest
            In the very end of harvest.
            Scarcity and want shall shun you.
            Ceres' blessing so is on you.

FERDINAND : This is a most majestic vision, and
    Harmonious charmingly. May I be bold
    To think these spirits?

PROSPERO :   Spirits, which by mine art   120
    I have from their confines called to enact
    My present fancies.

FERDINAND :   Let me live here ever;
    So rare a wondered father, and a wise
    Makes this place Paradise.

        [Juno and Ceres whisper, and send Iris on employment

PROSPERO :   Sweet now, silence.
    Juno and Ceres whisper seriously;
    There 's something else to do. Hush, and be mute,
    Or else our spell is marred.

IRIS : You nymphs, called Naiads, of the windring brooks,

130   *crisp*, curled.

132   *temperate*, modest.
       Should Iris make magical gestures or adopt any pose to summon
       the nymphs?

137–8 *encounter . . . footing*, take as partners in a country dance.
       Dancing in masques with both men and women symbolized
       union and harmony. Here the nymphs represent chastity and the
       harvesters fertility.

S.D.   *a graceful dance*. Cutts suggests that the music entitled 'Haymakers'
       Dance' in British Museum manuscript *Additional* 10444 may
       have been the music for this dance.

S.D.   *Prospero . . . speaks*. This suggests that Prospero's words break
       the charm. *hollow*, echoing. *heavily*, sorrowfully.

142   *avoid*, go away, withdraw.
143–4 *This . . . strongly*. What movements or gestures show this?
143   *passion*, deep feeling.
144   *works*, moves, agitates.

145   *distempered*, put out, disconcerted.

146–7 *You . . . sir*. Prospero recovers his self-control quickly, and seeing
       Ferdinand discomposed at events seeks to allay his anxiety.
146   *moved sort*, troubled state of mind.
148   *revels*, entertainment.

153   *great globe*, (a) the earth, (b) the universe or macrocosm.
154   *inherit*, occupy.

With your sedged crowns and ever-harmless looks,
Leave your crisp channels, and on this green land   130
Answer your summons; Juno does command.
Come temperate nymphs, and help to celebrate
A contract of true love. Be not too late.

Enter certain Nymphs

You sunburnt sicklemen of August weary,
Come hither from the furrow, and be merry.
Make holiday. Your rye-straw hats put on,
And these fresh nymphs encounter every one
In country footing.

*Enter certain Reapers, properly habited: they join with the Nymphs
in a graceful dance; towards the end whereof* PROSPERO *starts
suddenly, and speaks; after which, to a strange, hollow, and confused
noise, they heavily vanish*

PROSPERO: [*Aside*] I had forgot that foul conspiracy
   Of the beast Caliban and his confederates   140
   Against my life. The minute of their plot
   Is almost come. [*To the Spirits.*] Well done, avoid. No more.
FERDINAND: This is strange. Your father's in some passion
   That works him strongly.
MIRANDA: Never till this day
   Saw I him touched with anger so distempered.
PROSPERO: You do look, my son, in a moved sort,
   As if you were dismayed. Be cheerful sir.
   Our revels now are ended. These our actors,
   As I foretold you, were all spirits, and
   Are melted into air, into thin air;   150
   And like the baseless fabric of this vision,
   The cloud-capped towers, the gorgeous palaces,
   The solemn temples, the great globe itself,
   Yea, all which it inherit, shall dissolve,

155   *insubstantial pageant*, i.e. the masque presented by the spirits.

156   *rack*, cloud.

157   *little life*, (*a*) brief existence, (*b*) life as the microcosm in contrast with the great globe or macrocosm.

158   *rounded*, (*a*) completed, rounded off, (*b*) crowned. See *I Henry IV*, III. i, 244.

Some consider that this speech is inconsistent in that Prospero encourages Ferdinand to be cheerful and then gravely reminds him of the transitoriness of all human endeavours. Others think that it refers to the masque sets on the stage, or to the pageants that greeted James I on his arrival in London, or to the common lament for the departed glory of imperial Rome. It has even been suggested that it's only use is to fill in time while Ariel changes his costume!

The thought was frequently expressed—Spenser has a very similar passage in the *Ruins of Time*—as a reminder of the human condition brought about by the Fall. Prospero, as the representative of Providence, sums up the themes of metamorphosis, time, self-knowledge, society, illusion and reality within the framework of God's ordered creation. Neither the visionary blessing nor the island paradise are eternal.

160   *infirmity*, weakness.

163   *To . . . mind*. See I. ii, 176; V. i, 246.

164   *Come . . . Come.* According to Sisson Prospero turns from the lovers and summons Ariel who arrives while Prospero is in the act of speaking. Prospero thanks him and calls him closer. Another view is that 'I thank thee' is addressed to Ferdinand and Miranda for their good wishes, although admittedly 'you' would be expected in place of 'thee'.

165   *Thy . . . to.* 'Indicates the immediacy of his fusion with Prospero's thoughts' (Sisson).

166   *meet with*, deal with, encounter.

167-9 *when . . . thee.* Is this to demonstrate—Prospero's irascible temper, or Ariel's submission? Had Ariel failed in any way?

167   *presented*, either (*a*) acted, or (*b*) introduced. Perhaps the latter is the more likely view since it would have been difficult for Ceres to break away from her part to give Prospero warning.

170   *Say . . . varlets?* Is Prospero forgetful, or is this a linking device to give the impression of depth or of a life outside the stage?

172   *valour*, Dutch courage.

175   *tabor*, side drum.

And like this insubstantial pageant faded,
Leave not a rack behind. We are such stuff
As dreams are made on, and our little life
Is rounded with a sleep. Sir, I am vexed;
Bear with my weakness; my old brain is troubled.
Be not disturbed with my infirmity.   160
If you be pleased, retire into my cell,
And there repose: a turn or two I 'll walk
To still my beating mind.

FERDINAND: ⎫
                    ⎬   We wish your peace.   [*Exeunt*
MIRANDA: ⎭

PROSPERO: Come with a thought. I thank thee Ariel. Come.

Enter ARIEL

ARIEL: Thy thoughts I cleave to. What 's thy pleasure?
PROSPERO: Spirit,
   We must prepare to meet with Caliban.
ARIEL: Ay my commander, when I presented Ceres,
   I thought to have told thee of it; but I feared
   Lest I might anger thee.
PROSPERO: Say again, where didst thou leave these varlets?   170
ARIEL: I told you sir, they were red-hot with drinking;
   So full of valour that they smote the air
   For breathing in their faces; beat the ground
   For kissing of their feet; yet always bending
   Towards their project. Then I beat my tabor;

176   *unbacked*, unbroken.
177   *Advanced*, raised. See I. ii, 407.

179   *lowing*, i.e. of a mother cow.
180   *goss*, gorse.

182   *filthy-mantled*, covered with dirty green scum.

184   *O'erstunk their feet*, i.e. the stench of the pool outstank even that of their feet. *bird*. See V. i, 316.

186   *trumpery*, tawdry clothing.
187   *stale*, decoy.
     What is the point of this device—to distract the three plotters, to divert them from Prospero's cell, to show up their characters, to oppose appearance and reality?
189   *Nurture*, education, civilized training.
190   *Humanely*, (*a*) out of kindness, (*b*) humanly. *taken*, bestowed.
     Is Prospero regretful, embittered, or despairing?
191–2 *And . . . cankers*. Kermode notes the 'Platonic equation of spirit and body', i.e. that physical appearance reflects spiritual qualities. Some quote Essex's sneer at Elizabeth I, 'That she grew old and cankered, and that her mind was become as crooked as her carcase'.
192   *cankers*, becomes corrupt.

193   *line*, (*a*) lime-tree, (*b*) clothes line. See ll. 234–6. Editors dispute which is preferable.
S.D. Who leads? Where are Prospero and Ariel stationed?

194–5 *that . . . fall*. The mole's hearing is very sensitive, and his eyes appear to be covered with fur.

197   *played the Jack*, (*a*) tricked, (*b*) acted like a will-o'-the-wisp.

200   *take a displeasure*. Stephano affects kingly speech.

At which, like unbacked colts, they pricked their ears,
Advanced their eyelids, lifted up their noses
As they smelt music. So I charmed their ears
That calf-like they my lowing followed through
Toothed briers, sharp furzes, pricking goss and, thorns,   180
Which entered their frail shins. At last I left them
I' th' filthy-mantled pool beyond your cell,
There dancing up to th' chins, that the foul lake
O'erstunk their feet.

PROSPERO: This was well done, my bird.
Thy shape invisible retain thou still.
The trumpery in my house, go bring it hither,
For stale to catch these thieves.

ARIEL: I go, I go.   [*Exit*

PROSPERO: A devil, a born devil, on whose nature
Nurture can never stick; on whom my pains,
Humanely taken, all, all lost, quite lost;   190
And as with age his body uglier grows,
So his mind cankers. I will plague them all,
Even to roaring.

Enter ARIEL, *loaden with glistering apparel, &c*

Come, hang them on this line.

PROSPERO *and* ARIEL *remain, invisible. Enter* CALIBAN,
STEPHANO, *and* TRINCULO, *all wet*

CALIBAN: Pray you tread softly, that the blind mole may not
Hear a foot fall; we now are near his cell.

STEPHANO: Monster, your fairy, which you say is a harmless
fairy, has done little better than played the Jack with us.

TRINCULO: Monster, I do smell all horse-piss, at which my nose
is in great indignation.

STEPHANO: Do you hear, monster? If I should take a displeasure
against you, look you—

202 *Thou . . . monster.* Does Trinculo interrupt Stephano, or does Stephano fail to think of an appropriate punishment which Trinculo then supplies?

203–5 *Good . . . mischance.* Does Caliban kneel, fawn, cringe, remain standing?

205 *hoodwink*, cover from sight.

208 *disgrace and dishonour*, i.e. as true knights they have suffered the dishonour of losing their weapons.

210 *That's . . . wetting.* Dishonour or the loss of the sack?

212 *fetch off*, recover by a soldierly exploit. *o'er ears*, submerged, immersed.

214 *my king.* Is Caliban servile or is this an anticipation of Trinculo's allusion to ballad King Stephen in l. 224?

216 *good mischief.* The figure of speech concentrates and stresses the thought. *mischief*, crime, evil.

217–8 *I . . . foot-licker.* Does he lick Stephano's shoe?

219 *Give . . . hand.* Do they shake hands, or does Stephano raise him from his grovelling position?

221–2 *O . . . thee.* Trinculo's exclamations on seeing the clothes that Prospero and Ariel have hung up echo the ballad, 'Take thy old cloak about thee':

> King Stephen was a worthy peer,
> His breeches cost him but a crown,
> He held them sixpence all too dear,
> Therefore he called the tailor lown.

Is this allusion a jest at Stephano's expense, or intended ironically to put Stephano's royal pretensions into apt perspective?

225 *frippery*, an old clothes' shop, i.e. these are not trash but good clothes.

For Stephano and Trinculo the outward trappings of power are more important than power itself.

229 *The . . . fool.* Addressed to Trinculo, who first drew Stephano's attention to the clothes and diverted his 'bloody thoughts'.

230 *luggage*, burdensome, trumpery stuff. *Let 't alone.* The Folio has 'let's alone' which is possible, but Caliban may be repeating 'Let 't alone' (l. 223).

TRINCULO: Thou wert but a lost monster.   202

CALIBAN: Good my lord, give me thy favour still.
   Be patient, for the prize I'll bring thee to
   Shall hoodwink this mischance. Therefore speak softly.
   All's hushed as midnight yet.

TRINCULO: Ay, but to lose our bottles in the pool—

STEPHANO: There is not only disgrace and dishonour in that,
   monster, but an infinite loss.

TRINCULO: That's more to me than my wetting. Yet this is your
   harmless fairy, monster.

STEPHANO: I will fetch off my bottle, though I be o'er ears for
   my labour.   213

CALIBAN: Prithee, my king, be quiet. See'st thou here,
   This is the mouth o' th' cell. No noise, and enter.
   Do that good mischief which may make this island
   Thine own for ever, and I, thy Caliban,
   For aye thy foot-licker.

STEPHANO: Give me thy hand. I do begin to have bloody
   thoughts.

TRINCULO: O king Stephano, O peer! O worthy Stephano!
   Look what a wardrobe here is for thee.   222

CALIBAN: Let't alone, thou fool, it is but trash.

TRINCULO: O, ho, monster, we know what belongs to a
   frippery. O king Stephano!

STEPHANO: Put off that gown, Trinculo, by this hand I'll have
   that gown.

TRINCULO: Thy grace shall have it.

CALIBAN: The dropsy drown this fool. What do you mean
   To dote thus on such luggage? Let't alone,   230
   And do the murder first. If he awake,

232   *pinches*. Perhaps in view of 'stuff' a glance at 'pinches' = pleats or gathers in a garment.

233   *strange stuff*. Kermode notes that this 'refers back to the glistering apparel'. *stuff*, coarse material.

234–6 *Mistress . . . jerkin*. Obscure and possibly obscene puns.

234   *line*, (*a*) lime-tree, (*b*) clothes line, (*c*) ? loin, (*d*) equator.

235   *under the line*, south of the equator, below the loins.

236   *lose your hair*, i.e. on account of heat, fever, or venereal disease. *jerkin*, made of a furred skin.

237   *Do, do*. Perhaps 'Well done' or 'Good, good'. *steal*. Perhaps an echo of Prospero's 'stale' l. 187. Kokeritz, *Shakespeare's Pronunciation*, detects puns on 'stale' and 'steal' in *1 Henry IV*. *by . . . level*, according to rule, precisely. *an 't*, if it.

241   *pass of pate*, wit crack. *pass*, a thrust in fencing.

243   *lime*, bird-lime. A sticky substance smeared on twigs to catch birds. An extension of the 'line' quibble.

246   *barnacles*, barnacle-geese, popularly supposed to come from the barnacle shell-fish.

247   *With . . . low*. Low foreheads were regarded as ugly. See *Antony and Cleopatra*, III. iii, 32–3; *Two Gentlemen of Verona*, IV. iv, 189.

257   *dry convulsions*, severe wrenchings or spasms of pain.

258   *aged cramps*, cramps of old people.

259   *cat o' mountain*, leopard or panther.

      Why is this method used for disposing of the three plotters—to imply that like Actæon their desires pursue them in the shape of hounds, to appeal to James I's passion for dogs, to indicate their beast-like nature?

From toe to crown he 'll fill our skins with pinches,
Make us strange stuff.

STEPHANO : Be you quiet, monster. Mistress line, is not this my
jerkin? Now is the jerkin under the line. Now, jerkin, you are
like to lose your hair, and prove a bald jerkin.

TRINCULO : Do, do: we steal by line and level, an 't like your
grace.

STEPHANO : I thank thee for that jest; here 's a garment for 't. Wit
shall not go unrewarded while I am king of this country. 'Steal
by line and level' is an excellent pass of pate; there 's another
garment for 't.   242

TRINCULO : Monster, come put some lime upon your fingers,
and away with the rest.

CALIBAN : I will have none on 't. We shall lose our time,
And all be turned to barnacles, or to apes
With foreheads, villainous low.

STEPHANO : Monster, lay-to your fingers. Help to bear this
away where my hogshead of wine is, or I 'll turn you out of
my kingdom. Go to, carry this.   250

TRINCULO : And this.

STEPHANO : Ay, and this.

*A noise of hunters heard. Enter divers Spirits, in shape of dogs and
hounds, and hunt them about,* PROSPERO *and* ARIEL *setting
them on*

PROSPERO : Hey, Mountain, hey!

ARIEL : Silver! there it goes, Silver!

PROSPERO : Fury, Fury! There, Tyrant, there! Hark! Hark!
                    [*Caliban, Stephano, and Trinculo are driven out*
Go charge my goblins that they grind their joints
With dry convulsions, shorten up their sinews
With aged cramps, and more pinch-spotted make them
Than pard or cat o' mountain.

ARIEL :   Hark, they roar.

PROSPERO : Let them be hunted soundly. At this hour   260
    Lie at my mercy all mine enemies.
    Shortly shall all my labours end, and thou
    Shalt have the air at freedom. For a little
    Follow, and do me service.   [*Exeunt*

Before Prospero's cell

s.d.   Prospero and Ariel should make a ceremonial entry in full
       panoply to lead up to Prospero's ritual renunciation of his magical
       powers.

1   *project*, (*a*) plan, (*b*) projection, i.e. the casting of powder of the
       philosopher's stone into a crucible to transmute base metal to
       gold. *gather . . . head*, (*a*) come to the critical point in alchemical
       experiments, (*b*) of a boil raised to a head, ripe.

2   *crack*, i.e. like the shattering of retorts in alchemical experiments.

2–3   *time . . . carriage*, i.e. little remains to be done, and my work is on
       time.

10   *line-grove*, lime-tree grove. *weather-fends*, shelters from bad
       weather.

11   *your release*, released by you.

12   *distracted*, out of their senses.

17   *works*, moves, affects.

18   *affections*, feelings.

21   *touch*, sensitive feeling, awareness.

158

ACT FIVE

SCENE ONE

Enter PROSPERO *in his magic robes, and* ARIEL

PROSPERO: Now does my project gather to a head:
  My charms crack not; my spirits obey; and time
  Goes upright with his carriage. How 's the day?
ARIEL: On the sixth hour; at which time, my lord,
  You said our work should cease.
PROSPERO: I did say so,
  When first I raised the tempest. Say, my spirit,
  How fares the King and 's followers?
ARIEL: Confined together
  In the same fashion as you gave in charge,
  Just as you left them; all prisoners, sir,
  In the line-grove which weather-fends your cell;   10
  They cannot budge till your release. The King,
  His brother, and yours, abide all three distracted,
  And the remainder mourning over them,
  Brimful of sorrow and dismay; but chiefly
  Him that you termed, sir, 'The good old lord, Gonzalo';
  His tears run down his beard, like winter's drops
  From eaves of reeds. Your charm so strongly works 'em
  That if you now beheld them, your affections
  Would become tender.
PROSPERO: Dost thou think so, spirit?
ARIEL: Mine would, sir, were I human.
PROSPERO: And mine shall.   20
  Hast thou, which art but air, a touch, a feeling

The Tempest

22   *Of*, for.

23-4 *that . . . they*, who savours everything with as keen sensitivity as they do, has as deep feelings as they do.

24   *kindlier*, (*a*) with more fellow feeling, (*b*) more human-kind-like.

       Is Prospero influenced into being merciful by Ariel, has he all along decided on forgiving his enemies, is this a dramatic device to evaluate and make clear to the audience Prospero's attitude and intention?

25   *high*, great.

26-7 *Yet . . . part*. The supremacy of reason over emotion was a sign of greatness of mind.

27-8 *The . . . vengeance*, the finer deed is expressed through christian love and forbearance and not in exacting vengeance.

32   *And . . . themselves*. Perhaps in a double sense (*a*) be restored to their senses, (*b*) have a true knowledge of themselves.

33-50 *Ye . . . art*. Editors have remarked on the close resemblance of this passage to Medea's incantation in Ovid's *Metamorphoses*, Bk. VII, when she was preparing to renew Aeson's youth. See Introduction, p. 15. Does Prospero make any ritual gestures in this tremendous invocation?

36   *demi-puppets*, tiny elves.

37   *the . . . make*. The 'fairy rings' of folk-lore. It was believed that the rings of darkened grass where toadstools grow was caused by fairies dancing.

38   *Whereof . . . bites*. Sheep avoid grazing on fairy rings perhaps because of the toadstools.

39   *midnight mushrooms*, i.e. they appear to grow during darkness.

39-40 *that . . . curfew*, i.e. because they are then free to wander.

40   *curfew*, a bell rung in the evening to warn householders to extinguish their fires.

41   *masters*. Possibly 'instruments'. *bedimmed*, eclipsed.

42   *mutinous winds*, i.e. from the caves where they were supposed to be imprisoned.

47   *spurs*, lateral roots.

48-50 *Graves . . . art*. See Introduction, p. 15.

50-1 *But . . . abjure*. Any change of tone or speed of speaking? Any gestures?

50   *rough*, elemental, material.

51   *abjure*, i.e. what he achieved, his powers of conjuring. *required*, asked for.

53-4 *that . . . for*, which is the purpose of.

Of their afflictions, and shall not myself,
One of their kind, that relish all as sharply,
Passion as they, be kindlier moved than thou art?
Though with their high wrongs I am struck to th' quick,
Yet with my nobler reason, 'gainst my fury
Do I take part. The rarer action is
In virtue than in vengeance. They being penitent,
The sole drift of my purpose doth extend
Not a frown further. Go release them Ariel.   30
My charms I 'll break, their senses I 'll restore,
And they shall be themselves.
ARIEL: I 'll fetch them, sir.

                                                           [*Exit*

PROSPERO: Ye elves of hills, brooks, standing lakes, and groves,
    And ye that on the sands with printless foot
    Do chase the ebbing Neptune, and do fly him
    When he comes back; you demi-puppets that
    By moonshine do the green sour ringlets make,
    Whereof the ewe not bites; and you whose pastime
    Is to make midnight mushrooms, that rejoice
    To hear the solemn curfew; by whose aid—   40
    Weak masters though ye be—I have bedimmed
    The noontide sun, called forth the mutinous winds,
    And 'twixt the green sea and the azured vault
    Set roaring war. To the dread rattling thunder
    Have I given fire, and rifted Jove's stout oak
    With his own bolt. The strong-based promontory
    Have I made shake, and by the spurs plucked up
    The pine and cedar. Graves at my command
    Have waked their sleepers, oped, and let 'em forth
    By my so potent art. But this rough magic   50
    I here abjure; and when I have required
    Some heavenly music—which even now I do—
    To work mine end upon their senses that

                                    161

54   *charm*, music.

54-7   *I'll ... book.* Why does Prospero renounce his magical powers, because—they are invalid in orderly civilized society, he has achieved his aims, he has attained a state of virtue, the profession of magician was dangerous?

56   *And ... sound.* See III. iii, 100–2.

S.D.   *Solemn music.* What instruments—recorders, viols, lutes? Where are the players placed? *frantic gesture.* What would be suitable— hands beating head, staggering, disarranging clothes? *circle*, a magic circle traced on the ground within which magic operated most strongly.

58-9   *A ... fancy*, solemn music which is the best soother of mental distress.

60   *boiled*, i.e. sodden and lifeless. The Folio has 'boile' and it is possible to render it 'thy brains which, now useless, boil ...'. See *A Midsummer Night's Dream*, V. i, 4.

62   *Holy*, reverend, upright.

63-4   *even ... drops*, my eyes touched at the sight of your tears weep in sympathy.
       Prospero should move suitably to address Gonzalo, Alonso, Sebastian, and Antonio who stand rigid. Should they show any signs of animation?

66-8   *rising ... reason*, like the sun that drives away the darkness and the morning mists, the air-like vital spirits rise from the heart to clear the brain of the fog of ignorance.

70   *graces*, (*a*) virtues, (*b*) favours, kindnesses.

71   *Home*, in full.

74   *pinched*, by (*a*) pricking of conscience, (*b*) distracted mind.

74-5   *Flesh ... mine*, you, my brother, my own flesh and blood.
       Is Prospero grief-stricken, sarcastic, venomous, bitter, sorrowful, horrified?

75   *entertained*, nursed, cherished.

76   *remorse and nature*, pity and natural feelings.

77   *inward pinches*, bitings of conscience.

79-82 *Their ... muddy*, their powers of understanding, like the rising tide, come flooding back, and soon their reasoning faculties will be restored to their minds which are now confused and obscured.

This airy charm is for, I 'll break my staff,
Bury it certain fathoms in the earth,
And deeper than did ever plummet sound
I 'll drown my book.   [*Solemn music*

Enter ARIEL *before: then* ALONSO, *with a frantic gesture, attended
by* GONZALO; SEBASTIAN *and* ANTONIO *in like manner,
attended by* ADRIAN *and* FRANCISCO: *they all enter the circle
which* PROSPERO *had made, and there stand charmed; which*
PROSPERO *observing, speaks*

A solemn air, and the best comforter
To an unsettled fancy, cure thy brains,
Now useless, boiled within thy skull. There stand,   60
For you are spell-stopped.
Holy Gonzalo, honourable man,
Mine eyes, even sociable to the show of thine,
Fall fellowly drops. The charm dissolves apace,
And as the morning steals upon the night,
Melting the darkness, so their rising senses
Begin to chase the ignorant fumes that mantle
Their clearer reason. O good Gonzalo,
My true preserver, and a loyal sir
To him thou follow'st, I will pay thy graces   70
Home both in word and deed. Most cruelly
Didst thou, Alonso, use me and my daughter;
Thy brother was a furtherer in the act.
Thou art pinched for 't now Sebastian. Flesh and blood,
You, brother mine, that entertained ambition,
Expelled remorse and nature; who, with Sebastian—
Whose inward pinches therefore are most strong—
Would here have killed your King; I do forgive thee,
Unnatural though thou art. Their understanding
Begins to swell, and the approaching tide   80
Will shortly fill the reasonable shore

83   *That . . . me*, yet sees me or would recognize me even if he did.

85   *discase*, i.e. from his magic robes.
86   *sometime Milan*, formerly Duke of Milan.

88–94 *Where . . . bough.* What is the value of this song—to pass the time
       while Prospero attires himself, to confirm the theme of freedom,
       to mark the magical release of the courtiers from the charm, to
       herald his own release as Prospero's 'discasing' heralds the re-
       nouncing of his magical powers.
           What are the King and courtiers doing during this song and
       conversation—struggling to free themselves, stretching, rubbing
       their eyes, yawning, moving stiffly?

96   *so, so, so.* This way, that's right, well done! Prospero arranges his
       clothes and rapier.

101   *presently*, immediately.
102   *I . . . me.* See *2 Henry IV*, I. ii, 47.

That now lies foul and muddy. Not one of them
That yet looks on me, or would know me. Ariel,
Fetch me the hat and rapier in my cell.
I will discase me, and myself present
As I was sometime Milan. Quickly spirit,
Thou shalt ere long be free.

ARIEL *sings, and helps to attire him*

Where the bee sucks, there suck I.
In a cowslip's bell I lie;
There I couch when owls do cry.   90
On the bat's back I do fly
After summer merrily.
Merrily, merrily shall I live now
Under the blossom that hangs on the bough.

PROSPERO: Why, that's my dainty Ariel. I shall miss thee,
But yet thou shalt have freedom. So, so, so.
To the King's ship, invisible as thou art.
There shalt thou find the mariners asleep
Under the hatches. The master and the boatswain
Being awake, enforce them to this place,   100
And presently, I prithee.
ARIEL: I drink the air before me, and return
Or ere your pulse twice beat.   [*Exit*
GONZALO: All torment, trouble, wonder and amazement
Inhabits here. Some heavenly power guide us
Out of this fearful country.
PROSPERO: Behold, sir King,
The wronged Duke of Milan, Prospero.
For more assurance that a living prince
Does now speak to thee, I embrace thy body;
And to thee and thy company I bid   110
A hearty welcome.

165

111– *Whether ... blood*. The tempo and tone of Alonso's speech reveal
14 his bemused state.
112 *trifle*, trick. *abuse*, deceive.
113– *Thy ... blood*. What movements or actions?
14

116– *This ... story*, this must demand—if all this has any reality at all—
17 a most strange explanation.
118 *Thy ... resign*, i.e. give up demands for tribute (I. ii, 124).
119 *wrongs*, wrongdoings against you.

120 *noble friend*, Gonzalo.

123–4 *taste ... isle*, are under the influence of some of the illusions here.
Some see a glance at the banquet episode for 'subtle' was a word
used to describe highly ornate and elaborate confectionery.
125 *certain*, real.
126 *brace*. Contemptuous.

127 *pluck*, call down.
128 *justify*, prove.

129 *No*. Prospero overhears Sebastian's aside.

131 *even infect*, indeed befoul. Emphatic.
132 *rankest*, most corrupt. Perhaps a glance at the meaning 'over-
grown, proud' connected with ambition.
134 *Thou must restore*. Antonio does not reply. Does he display con-
trition or sullen resentment by some gesture or action?

ALONSO: Whether thou be'st he or no,
Or some enchanted trifle to abuse me,
As late I have been, I not know. Thy pulse
Beats, as of flesh and blood. And, since I saw thee,
Th' affliction of my mind amends, with which,
I fear a madness held me. This must crave—
An if this be at all—a most strange story.
Thy dukedom I resign, and do entreat
Thou pardon me my wrongs. But how should Prospero
Be living and be here?

PROSPERO: First, noble friend,   120
Let me embrace thine age, whose honour cannot
Be measured or confined.

GONZALO: Whether this be
Or be not, I 'll not swear.

PROSPERO: You do yet taste
Some subtilties o' th' isle, that will not let you
Believe things certain. Welcome, my friends all.
[*Aside to Sebastian and Antonio*] But you, my brace of lords,
were I so minded,
I here could pluck his highness' frown upon you
And justify you traitors. At this time
I will tell no tales.

SEBASTIAN: [*Aside*] The devil speaks in him.

PROSPERO: No.
For you, most wicked sir, whom to call brother   130
Would even infect my mouth, I do forgive
Thy rankest fault—all of them; and require
My dukedom of thee, which perforce I know,
Thou must restore.

ALONSO: If thou be'st Prospero,
Give us particulars of thy preservation;
How thou hast met us here, who three hours since
Were wrecked upon this shore; where I have lost—

139   *woe*, sorry.

142   *of . . . grace*, by whose gentle mercy.
143   *sovereign*, most healing.

145   *late*, recent.
145–6 *supportable . . . loss*, to make bearable the loss of one so precious.
146   *means much weaker*. Alonso still has a daughter, Claribel.

154   *do . . . admire*, are so greatly astonished.
        Do any postures, gestures or movements by the lords lead up to
        Prospero's words?
155   *devour*, overpower, swallow up.
157   *natural breath*, ordinary speech.

163   *chronicle . . . day*, story that will take some days to tell.
164   *Not . . . breakfast*, not a brief story to be told at one sitting.

How sharp the point of this remembrance is—
My dear son Ferdinand.

PROSPERO: I am woe for 't, sir.

ALONSO: Irreparable is the loss, and patience   140
    Says it is past her cure.

PROSPERO: I rather think
    You have not sought her help, of whose soft grace
    For the like loss I have her sovereign aid,
    And rest myself content.

ALONSO: You the like loss?

PROSPERO: As great to me as late; and, supportable
    To make the dear loss, have I means much weaker
    Than you may call to comfort you, for I
    Have lost my daughter.

ALONSO: A daughter?
    O heavens, that they were living both in Naples,
    The king and queen there. That they were, I wish   150
    Myself were mudded in that oozy bed
    Where my son lies. When did you lose your daughter?

PROSPERO: In this last tempest. I perceive these lords
    At this encounter do so much admire,
    That they devour their reason, and scarce think
    Their eyes do offices of truth, their words
    Are natural breath. But howsoe'er you have
    Been justled from your senses, know for certain
    That I am Prospero, and that very duke
    Which was thrust forth of Milan, who most strangely   160
    Upon this shore, where you were wrecked, was landed,
    To be the lord on 't. No more yet of this;
    For 'tis a chronicle of day by day,
    Not a relation for a breakfast, nor
    Befitting this first meeting. Welcome, sir,
    This cell 's my court. Here have I few attendants,
    And subjects none abroad. Pray you look in.

170   *a wonder*, a marvel, i.e. Miranda.

S.D.   Ferdinand and Miranda are in either a 'mansion' projecting from the rear wall, or a curtained recess in the wall. In the Banqueting Hall performance probably they were in Prospero's cave back stage. *playing at chess*. Chess was very much a royal or aristocratic game symbolic of government.

173   *for the world*, on any account.

174   *Yes . . . wrangle*, Yes, for a mere score of kingdoms you would cheat. Miranda quibbles on 'world'.

176   *vision . . . island*, illusion.

177   *A . . . miracle*. Is this a sign of virtue in Sebastian?

180   *compass thee about*, surround you, be upon you.

181   *Arise*. Is Ferdinand kneeling or still sitting?

182–4   *How . . . in't*. Is this ironical in that there are present two would-be murderers and a usurper, are all reclaimed and purged of sin, has the new world redressed the balance of the old, is it a justification of the civilized christian social order?

183   *mankind*, (*a*) human beings, (*b*) men (man-kind). *brave*, fine.

184   *'Tis . . . thee*. Is this—factual, ironic, sarcastic, bitter?

186   *three hours*. Again a reminder of the time. See l. 223.

187   *goddess*. See I. ii, 420–1.

188–9   *mortal . . . mine*. A play on the contradictory words.

189   *immortal Providence*. See I. ii, 159.

My dukedom since you have given me again,
I will requite you with as good a thing;
At least bring forth a wonder, to content ye   170
As much as me my dukedom.

Here Prospero discovers FERDINAND *and* MIRANDA *playing
at chess*

MIRANDA: Sweet lord, you play me false.
FERDINAND: No my dearest love,
  I would not for the world.
MIRANDA: Yes, for a score of kingdoms you should wrangle,
  And I would call it fair play.
ALONSO: If this prove
  A vision of the island, one dear son
  Shall I twice lose.
SEBASTIAN: A most high miracle.
FERDINAND: Though the seas threaten, they are merciful.
  I have cursed them without cause.   [*Kneels*
ALONSO: Now all the blessings
  Of a glad father compass thee about.   180
  Arise, and say how thou camest here.
MIRANDA: O wonder!
  How many goodly creatures are there here.
  How beauteous mankind is. O brave new world
  That has such people in 't!
PROSPERO: 'Tis new to thee.
ALONSO: What is this maid with whom thou wast at play?
  Your eld'st acquaintance cannot be three hours.
  Is she the goddess that hath severed us,
  And brought us thus together?
FERDINAND: Sir, she is mortal;
  But by immortal Providence she 's mine.
  I chose her when I could not ask my father   190
  For his advice, nor thought I had one. She

193   *renown*, (*a*) praise, (*b*) mention.

196   *hers*, i.e. father.
197-8 *But . . . forgiveness*. Any gesture or movement?

198   *There, sir, stop*. Any movement or action?

200   *heaviness*, sorrow.

202   *crown*, Symbol of royal united rule. Any gesture?

205   *Milan*, Prospero.

212–   *and . . . own*. See Introduction, pp. 11-12, for the theme of 'Know
13   thyself'. How are they grouped to give effect to this exultation?

214   *still embrace*, for ever cling to.

s.d.   What are Ariel's movements and gestures to bring in the seamen?
      How do they come—entranced, bemused, by music, sleep-
      walking, shepherded, driven? *amazedly*. Kermode quotes *A Mid-
      summer Night's Dream*, IV. i, 150–1. 'My lord I shall reply amazedly,
      Half asleep, half waking'.

Is daughter to this famous Duke of Milan,
Of whom so often I have heard renown,
But never saw before; of whom I have
Received a second life; and second father
This lady makes him to me.

ALONSO: I am hers.
But O, how oddly will it sound that I
Must ask my child forgiveness.

PROSPERO: There, sir, stop.
Let us not burden our remembrance with
A heaviness that's gone.

GONZALO: I have inly wept,   200
Or should have spoke ere this. Look down you gods,
And on this couple drop a blessed crown;
For it is you that have chalked forth the way
Which brought us hither.

ALONSO: I say Amen, Gonzalo.

GONZALO: Was Milan thrust from Milan, that his issue
Should become kings of Naples? O rejoice
Beyond a common joy, and set it down
With gold on lasting pillars. In one voyage
Did Claribel her husband find at Tunis,
And Ferdinand, her brother, found a wife,   210
Where he himself was lost, Prospero his dukedom
In a poor isle, and all of us ourselves
When no man was his own.

ALONSO: [*To Ferdinand and Miranda*] Give me your hands.
Let grief and sorrow still embrace his heart
That doth not wish you joy.

GONZALO: Be it so, Amen.

Enter ARIEL, *with the* Master *and* Boatswain *amazedly
following*

O look sir, look, sir. Here is more of us.

218   *blasphemy.* See 'malice' I. ii, 367, 'diligence' l. 241. See note to I. i, 31.

219   *swear'st grace o'erboard,* swearest so wickedly that grace was driven from the ship and therefore doomed the ship.

223   *three glasses since,* i.e. three hours ago.

224   *tight . . . rigged,* sound, ready and well-rigged.

226   *tricksy,* (*a*) full of tricks, (*b*) clever, (*c*) pretty.

227   *strengthen,* increase.

232   *several,* differing.

234   *moe,* more.

236   *in . . . trim,* in excellent shape, completely intact. *freshly,* again, afresh.

238   *Capering . . . her,* dancing for joy at the sight of her. *On a trice,* in an instant.

239   *Even . . . dream.* See note to 'amazedly' s.D. *them,* the crew.

240   *moping,* (*a*) gloomy, sorrowful, (*b*) stupefied.

241   *diligence,* quick, industrious spirit.

242   *maze,* winding paths.

243-4 *more . . . of.* Alonso repeats his thought of l. 227.

244   *conduct,* guider.

I prophesied, if a gallows were on land,
This fellow could not drown. Now blasphemy,
That swear'st grace o'erboard, not an oath on shore?
Hast thou no mouth by land? What is the news?   220
BOATSWAIN: The best news is, that we have safely found
    Our King and company; the next, our ship,
    Which but three glasses since, we gave out split,
    Is tight and yare and bravely rigged, as when
    We first put out to sea.
ARIEL [*Aside to Prospero*] Sir, all this service
    Have I done since I went.
PROSPERO: [*Aside to Ariel*] My tricksy spirit.
ALONSO: These are not natural events, they strengthen
    From stranger to stranger. Say, how came you hither?
BOATSWAIN: If I did think, sir, I were well awake,
    I 'ld strive to tell you. We were dead of sleep,   230
    And—how we know not—all clapped under hatches,
    Where, but even now with strange and several noises
    Of roaring, shrieking, howling, jingling chains,
    And moe diversity of sounds, all horrible,
    We were awaked; straightway, at liberty;
    Where we, in all her trim, freshly beheld
    Our royal, good, and gallant ship; our master
    Capering to eye her. On a trice, so please you,
    Even in a dream, were we divided from them,
    And were brought moping hither.
ARIEL   [*Aside to Prospero*]   Was 't well done?   240
PROSPERO: [*Aside to Ariel*] Bravely, my diligence. Thou shalt
    be free.
ALONSO: This is as strange a maze as e'er men trod,
    And there is in this business more than nature
    Was ever conduct of. Some oracle
    Must rectify our knowledge.
PROSPERO: Sir, my liege,

175

246   *infest*, vex. *beating on*. See I. ii, 176; IV. i, 163.

247   *picked*, chosen.

248   *single*, detached, private. *resolve you*, explain to you.

249   *which . . . probable*, and it shall appear demonstrably true to you. *probable*, provable.

251   *well*, as being well.

253   *How . . . sir?* What gestures or actions by Alonso prompt this inquiry?

255   *odd*, stray.

S.D.   How does Ariel drive them—with a whip or goad, shoving them, with barking?
       Their attire should be odd, bizarre (see ll. 264–6).

256   *Every . . . himself.* Perhaps Stephano considers that the whole world has become topsy-turvy and he inverts the common phrase: 'Every man for himself'.

257   *Coragio*, cheer up, courage. *bully-monster*, my fine monster.
       Caliban (see ll. 262–3) is cowering away in fear.

259   *true spies*, eyes that see correctly. Any gesture?

261   *Setebos*, Sycorax's god. (I. ii, 373).

262   *How . . . is*, i.e. as he was 'sometime Milan' (l. 86). Caliban, too, sees a 'brave new world'.

265   *Will . . . 'em*, i.e. for a freak show.

266   *plain fish*, Caliban. See II. ii, 23.

267   *badges*, (a) coats of arms on livery, (b) appearance. Stephano and Trinculo as servants of Alonso should be wearing his livery bearing his coat of arms. The clothes they had stolen would have different coats of arms or none at all and would demonstrate that they were stolen. On the other hand Prospero may be speaking generally. 'Look at the appearance of these men. Do they look like honest men?'

268   *true*, honest. *This*, as for this.

Do not infest your mind with beating on
The strangeness of this business; at picked leisure,
Which shall be shortly, single I 'll resolve you,
Which to you shall seem probable, of every
These happened accidents; till when, be cheerful,   250
And think of each thing well. [*Aside to Ariel*] Come hither
    spirit:
Set Caliban and his companions free;
Untie the spell. [*Exit Ariel*] How fares my gracious sir?
There are yet missing of your company
Some few odd lads that you remember not.

Enter ARIEL, *driving in* CALIBAN, STEPHANO, *and*
TRINCULO, *in their stolen apparel*

STEPHANO: Every man shift for all the rest, and let no man take
    care for himself; for all is but fortune. Coragio bully-monster,
    coragio!
TRINCULO: If these be true spies which I wear in my head,
    here's a goodly sight.   260
CALIBAN: O Setebos, these be brave spirits indeed.
    How fine my master is. I am afraid
    He will chastise me.
SEBASTIAN: Ha, ha!
    What things are these, my lord Antonio?
    Will money buy 'em?
ANTONIO: Very like. One of them
    Is a plain fish, and no doubt marketable.
PROSPERO: Mark but the badges of these men, my lords,
    Then say if they be true. This mis-shapen knave,
    His mother was a witch, and one so strong
    That could control the moon, make flows and ebbs,   270

177

271 *deal . . . power*, do things normally attributable to the moon, work the effects of the moon's power outside the limits of her authority.

272 *demi-devil*, i.e. son of the Devil and a mortal (witch).

275 *this . . . darkness*, i.e. creature born of evil.

279 *reeling ripe*, full and staggering.

280 *grand*, mighty, powerful. *gilded*, flushed, ruddied their faces.

281 *pickle*, (*a*) mess, (*b*) soaking in liquor.

282-3 *I . . . fly-blowing*, he is now preserved in alcohol and is pickled meat on which flies will not lay eggs.

286 *a cramp*, a mass of cramps, one huge cramp. It has been noted that this may be a glance at 'stefano' a Neapolitan word for a 'stomach'.

288 *sore*, (*a*) harsh, (*b*) sorry, (*c*) suffering.

290-1 *He . . . shape*. The platonic correlation between form and mind. See I. ii, 456-8.

295 *grace*, pardon.

297 *dull fool*, witless clown. Is this true of Trinculo?

And deal in her command without her power.
These three have robbed me, and this demi-devil—
For he 's a bastard one—had plotted with them
To take my life. Two of these fellows you
Must know and own; this thing of darkness I
Acknowledge mine.

CALIBAN: I shall be pinched to death.

ALONSO: Is not this Stephano, my drunken butler?

SEBASTIAN: He is drunk now. Where had he wine?

ALONSO: And Trinculo is reeling ripe. Where should they
Find this grand liquor that hath gilded 'em?   280
How cam'st thou in this pickle?

TRINCULO: I have been in such a pickle since I saw you last that,
I fear me, will never out of my bones. I shall not fear fly-
blowing.

SEBASTIAN: Why how now Stephano.

STEPHANO: O touch me not, I am not Stephano, but a cramp.

PROSPERO: You 'd be king o' th' isle, sirrah?

STEPHANO: I should have been a sore one then.

ALONSO: This is a strange thing as e'er I look'd on.

                                        [*Pointing to Caliban*

PROSPERO: He is as disproportioned in his manners   290
As in his shape. Go sirrah, to my cell,
Take with you your companions. As you look
To have my pardon, trim it handsomely.

CALIBAN: Ay, that I will. And I 'll be wise hereafter,
And seek for grace. What a thrice-double ass
Was I to take this drunkard for a god,
And worship this dull fool.

PROSPERO: Go to, away.

ALONSO: Hence, and bestow your luggage where you found it.

SEBASTIAN: Or stole it rather.   [*Exeunt Caliban, Stephano, and
                                                    Trinculo*

PROSPERO: Sir, I invite your Highness, and your train   300

302   *waste*, spend.

305   *accidents*, happenings.

311   *Every ... grave*, i.e. I shall prepare myself for death. See Introduction, p. 10.

313   *Take ... strangely*, make strange hearing. *deliver*, tell.

314   *gales*, breezes.
315   *sail so expeditious*, so swift a sailing. *that shall*, that you shall.

317   *elements*, i.e. the air. How does Ariel depart—with ceremony, up to the 'heavens', by trap through the floor, by cloud machine?

10   *With ... hands*, i.e. by the sound of your applause which will break the spell.

To my poor cell, where you shall take your rest
For this one night, which, part of it, I 'll waste
With such discourse as, I not doubt, shall make it
Go quick away; the story of my life,
And the particular accidents gone by
Since I came to this isle. And in the morn
I 'll bring you to your ship, and so to Naples,
Where I have hope to see the nuptial
Of these our dear-beloved solemnized;
And thence retire me to my Milan, where   310
Every third thought shall be my grave.

ALONSO: I long
To hear the story of your life, which must
Take the ear strangely.

PROSPERO: I 'll deliver all,
And promise you calm seas, auspicious gales,
And sail so expeditious that shall catch
Your royal fleet far off. [*Aside to Ariel*] My Ariel, chick,
That is thy charge. Then to the elements
Be free, and fare thou well. Please you draw near.

                                                        [*Exeunt*

EPILOGUE

SPOKEN BY PROSPERO

Now my charms are all o'erthrown,
And what strength I have's mine own,
Which is most faint. Now't is true
I must be here confined by you,
Or sent to Naples. Let me not,
Since I have my dukedom got,
And pardoned the deceiver, dwell
In this bare island by your spell;
But release me from my bands
With the help of your good hands.   10

11   *Gentle breath*, i.e. favourable comment.

12   *project*. Perhaps an echo of V. i, 1.

13–18 *Now . . . faults.* Is this—the request of a white magician now
       devoid of his powers pleading for prayers for his soul, an apology
       to James I for dabbling in magic, an allusion to Shakespeare's
       retirement to Stratford, an appeal for applause?

Gentle breath of yours my sails
Must fill, or else my project fails,
Which was to please. Now I want
Spirits to enforce, art to enchant,
And my ending is despair,
Unless I be relieved by prayer,
Which pierces so, that it assaults
Mercy itself, and frees all faults.
As you from crimes would pardoned be,
Let your indulgence set me free.   20

                                              [*Exit*

APPENDICES

I

NOTE ON THE DATE OF THE PLAY

P. F. CRANEFIELD and W. Federn in the *Shakespeare Quarterly*, 1963, pp. 90-2, note that the reference to 'wallets of flesh' (III. iii, 46) was most probably taken either from Ortelius, *The Theatre of the Whole World*, 1606, or from Boemus, *The Manners, Laws, and Customs of All Nations*, 1611. The relevant passage in Boemus is: 'But the Stirii be a more rude and rustical kind of people, having marvellous great throats, yea their throat boles are so big as they are an impediment unto their speech, and that which is more (if it be truly reported of them) the women that give suck will cast their throats behind their backs like a wallet, to the end they should not hinder their children in their sucking'. Ortelius has the same description, ultimately derived from the early foreign editions of Boemus, with the variation, 'like a sack or wallet'. It is quite possible that Gonzalo's commonwealth although it owes much to Montaigne, may also owe something to the preface of Boemus' work. There the account of the primitive conditions of mankind is very much as described by Gonzalo, and indeed contains matters occurring in both but not found in Montaigne. An earlier version of Boemus' work, *The Fardle of Fashions*, 1563, has the same basic preface, but Aston's translation in the 1611 version seems nearer to Shakespeare.

If Shakespeare did draw on *The Manners, Laws, and Customs of All Nations* then, as presumably the date is 1611 old style, the book was not published before 25 March, and *The Tempest* would then have been composed after that date.

II

INFLUENCE OF THE ÆNEID

No source story for *The Tempest* has been discovered.

In view of Shakespeare's well-known reliance on existing stories or histories for the plots of his plays, this is unusual. The intense search for a source story has produced a number of claimants, but although each contains incidents or characters similar to those in *The Tempest* no direct relationship has been established. What is made clear, however, is that the matter of *The Tempest* is compounded of incidents, themes, and characters which are the common property of folk tales, ballads, fairy stories and romances widely spread over western Europe. There is little point, therefore, in describing a German play, stories from Spain, *scenari* from the Italian *Commedia dell'Arte*, Italian epic of Ariosto, Greek romance, since it cannot be shown that Shakespeare was directly influenced by any of them.

The parallels drawn between *The Tempest* and the *Æneid* on the other hand are in some interesting ways different in kind from those of other claimants. Although Kermode notes the 'strong echoes of the *Æneid*', and his 'feeling that Shakespeare has Virgil in mind', he appears not to accept the wider parallels of construction.

The resemblances were first pointed out by R. S. Conway in a lecture printed in *New Studies of a Great Inheritance*, 1921. Substantially the same points were made by J. M. Nosworthy—apparently unaware of Conway's lecture—in *Review of English Studies*, XXIV, Oct. 1948, 281–94, to which a few further details are here added.

That Shakespeare had the *Æneid* in mind seems indisputable. Ariel's 'eldest of furies' performance as a harpy is based on the speech of Celæno, the harpy, in *Æneid* III; there is direct reference to Dido in II. i, 72–81, 93–4, and editors for the most part accept the echoes of the *Æneid* in description of Juno's gait and Iris' wings in the masque.

The Tempest differs from Shakespeare's other romance plays and from romantic narratives in its construction, which observes the classical unities of time, place, and action according to renaissance interpretation of them. Instead of a chronological unfolding of the events of many years with a Chorus to tell the audience of the passing of time, these events are summed up by Prospero's narration in I. ii, which follows the initial dramatic action. Shakespeare had used the device early in his career in the *Comedy of Errors*, a comedy of intrigue, but not a romance. Something similar in construction and in incident was however available to him in the *Æneid*.

Action in both the *Æneid* and *The Tempest* begins with a storm at sea, supernaturally raised at Juno's command by Æolus, god of the winds in the former, and by Ariel, 'an airy spirit' at Prospero's command in the latter. The fleets of Alonso and Æneas are scattered. Neptune calms the waters enabling Æneas with seven ships to take refuge in a hidden rock-enclosed inlet, while Ariel hides Alonso's ship in a 'deep nook' and calms the storm. Both ships and men are supernaturally preserved. Miranda's tearful plea to her father to save the ship and the lives of the voyagers is similar to Venus' tearful plea to her father Jupiter for the safety of the Trojans. Both are assured that no harm has been done, that the voyagers are safe and that the consequences will be favourable to Venus and to Miranda. Æneas wandering with Achates meets his mother Venus disguised as a huntress. He addresses her as a virgin and a goddess, the latter honour she disclaims, just as Ferdinand on meeting Miranda asks if she is a virgin and assumes that she is a goddess, an honour that she too disclaims. Venus describes how Dido escaped from the treachery of her brother who had murdered her husband and seized the throne by taking ship and treasure and sailing to Carthage where she established a city. Dido's situation is similar to that of Prospero who was supplanted by his brother, set adrift in a boat, and arrived to make his kingdom in the island. Miranda first seeing Ferdinand takes him for a spirit. Dido first sees Æneas 'god-like' by his mother's powers.

The direct reference to Dido, while making a distinction between Dido and Claribel, does serve to point a parallel between the two works. Æneas' men, who offend the harpies and are therefore threatened by the harpy-fury Celæno, plead for pardon. Likewise Alonso, Antonio, and Sebastian, the three men of sin are threatened by Ariel as a harpy unless they repent and flee distracted. Here Shakespeare has clearly drawn a parallel between his play and the *Æneid*.

III

NOTES ON SOME OF THE SONGS
AND MUSIC

Two songs in the play have settings by Robert Johnson, lutanist, and were almost certainly used in the first productions of the play. The songs are 'Full fathom five', and 'Where the bee sucks' and their musical arrangement was first printed in John Wilson's *Cheerful Ayres*, 1659.

A manuscript, *Additional* 10444, in the British Museum contains a dance entitled 'The Tempest' which has been attributed to Robert Johnson. It possibly belongs to the dance of the Shapes bringing in the banquet. Another piece of music called 'A Masque' follows and Cutts suggests that its short length makes it suitable for the entry of Iris (IV. i, 60). Finally, a further piece the 'Haymaker's Dance' may well be the 'graceful dance' of the reapers and nymphs.

IV

SHAKESPEARE'S THEATRE

ALTHOUGH the evidence for the design of Elizabethan theatres is incomplete and conflicting, and although there were certainly differences of construction and arrangement, the following account, it is hoped, will give a reasonable outline.

The first public theatres in London were built during Shakespeare's lifetime. According to some they embodied in their design and construction the experience and practice of the medieval and Tudor play productions in inn yards, booth stages, and pageant wagons. Recently Glynne Wickham has argued strongly against this view, claiming that the game-houses, tournament arenas, banqueting chamber and town-hall provide the basis for Elizabethan stages both public or in banqueting rooms (*Early English Stages*, II, Pt. 1, p. 267).

From square, circular or hexagonal theatre walls tiered with galleries for spectators, the Elizabethan stage jutted out over six feet above ground level and occupied about half the floor space where the spectators could stand on three sides of it. The stage of the Fortune theatre was 43 feet × 27 feet and the floor area in which it stood was 55 feet × 55 feet. At the back of the stage the lowest tier of spectators' galleries gave place to a curtained recess or inner stage, a study or discovery space, used for interior scenes. Another view is that there was no recess, but a curtained space under a canopy in front of the rear wall of the stage. On either side were dressing rooms from which entrance doors opened on to the stage. The first floor gallery behind the stage was used for scenes in the play; a second floor gallery or room was used by musicians. Above the balcony and covering the rear portion of the stage was a canopy or roof painted blue and adorned with stars sometimes supported by pillars from the stage. There were trap-doors in the stage and frequently a low rail around it.

The pillars, canopy, railings, and back stage were painted and adorned. If a tragedy was to be performed, the stage was hung with black, but there was no stage setting in the modern fashion.

There were stage properties usually of the kind that could be easily pushed on and off the stage. Records of the time mention a mossy bank,

Courtesy of the British Council

MODEL OF AN ELIZABETHAN THEATRE
by Richard Southern

a wall, a bed, trees, arbours, thrones, tents, rock, tomb, hell-mouth, a cauldron; on the other hand tents, pavilions, and mansions may have been permanent 'sets' in some historical plays. These structures varied in size for a small one may have sufficed for the tomb in *Romeo and Juliet*, but the tent representing the Queen's chamber in Peele's *Edward I* contained six adults and a bed, as Armstrong pointed out. On the whole properties were limited to essentials although the popularity of the private masques with their painted canvas sets encouraged increasing elaboration of scenery and spectacle during the reign of James I.

There was no limitation to the display of rich and gorgeous costumes in the current fashion of the day. The more magnificent and splendid the better; indeed the costumes must have been the most expensive item in the requirements of the company. An occasional attempt was made at period costume, but normally plays were produced in Elizabethan garments without any suspicion of the oddness that strikes us when we read of Cæsar entering 'in his nightshirt' or Cleopatra calling on Charmian to cut the lace of what we may call her corsets. High rank was marked by magnificence of dress, a trade or calling by functional clothes. Feste, the clown, would wear the traditional fool's coat or petticoat of motley, a coarse cloth of mixed yellow and green. The coat was buttoned from the neck to the girdle from which hung a wooden dagger, its skirts voluminous with capacious pockets in which Feste might 'impetticoat' any 'gratillity'. Ghosts, who appear in a number of plays, wore a kind of leathern smock. Oberon and magicians such as Prospero wore, in the delightful phrase and spelling of the records, 'a robe for to goo invisibell'.

The actors formed companies under the patronage of noblemen for protection against a civic law condemning them as 'rogues, vagabonds and sturdy beggars' to severe punishment. They were the servants of their patron and wore his livery. The company was a co-operative society, its members jointly owned the property and shared the profits; thus Shakespeare's plays were not his to use as he liked, they belonged to his company, the Lord Chamberlain's Men. This company, honoured by James I when it became the King's Men, was the most successful company of the period. It had a number of distinguished actors, it achieved more Court performances than any other company, and it performed in the best London theatre, the Globe, until it was burnt down during a performance of *Henry VIII* in 1613. Women were not allowed on the public stage, although they performed in masques and theatricals in private houses. Boys, therefore, were apprenticed to the leading actors and took the female parts.

The audience in the public theatres was drawn from all classes. There were courtiers and inns of court men who appreciated intricate word play, mythological allusions and the technique of sword play; there were the 'groundlings' who liked jigs, horse-play and flamboyance of speech and spectacle; and there were the citizens who appreciated the romantic stories, the high eloquence of patriotic plays and moral sentiments. A successful play would have something for all. Sometimes gallants would sit on a stool on the stage and behave rather like the courtiers in *A Midsummer Night's Dream* V.i, or *Love's Labour's Lost*, V.ii. The 'groundlings' too were likely to be troublesome and noisy. They could buy bottled-beer, oranges, and nuts for their comfort; but it is noted to their credit that when Falstaff appeared on the stage, so popular was he that they stopped cracking nuts! They applauded a well delivered speech; they hissed a boring play; they even rioted and severely damaged one theatre. Shakespeare's plays however were popular among all classes: at Court they

did so take Eliza and our James,

and elsewhere in the public theatre they outshone the plays of other dramatists. Any play of his was assured of a 'full house'. An ardent theatre-goer of the day praising Shakespeare's plays above those of other dramatists wrote:

> When let but Falstaff come,
> Hal, Poins, the rest, you scarce shall have a room,
> All is so pester'd; let but Beatrice
> And Benedick be seen, lo in a trice
> The cockpit, galleries, boxes, all are full
> To hear Malvolio, that cross-garter'd gull.

Shakespeare's Works

The year of composition of only a few of Shakespeare's plays can be determined with certainty. The following list is based on current scholarly opinion.

The plays marked with an asterisk were not included in the First Folio edition of Shakespeare's plays (1623) which was prepared by Heminge and Condell, Shakespeare's fellow actors. Shakespeare's part in them has been much debated.

1590–1   2 Henry VI, 3 Henry VI.
1591–2   1 Henry VI.
1592–3   Richard III, Comedy of Errors.
1593–4   Titus Andronicus, Taming of the Shrew, Sir Thomas More* (Part authorship. Four manuscript pages presumed to be in Shakespeare's hand).
1594–5   Two Gentlemen of Verona, Love's Labour's Lost, Romeo and Juliet, Edward III* (Part authorship).
1595–6   Richard II, A Midsummer Night's Dream.
1596–7   King John, Merchant of Venice, Love's Labour Won (Not extant. Before 1598).
1597–8   1 Henry IV, 2 Henry IV, The Merry Wives of Windsor.
1598–9   Much Ado About Nothing, Henry V.
1599–1600   Julius Caesar, As You Like It.
1600–1   Hamlet, Twelfth Night.
1601–2   Troilus and Cressida.
1602–3   All's Well that Ends Well.